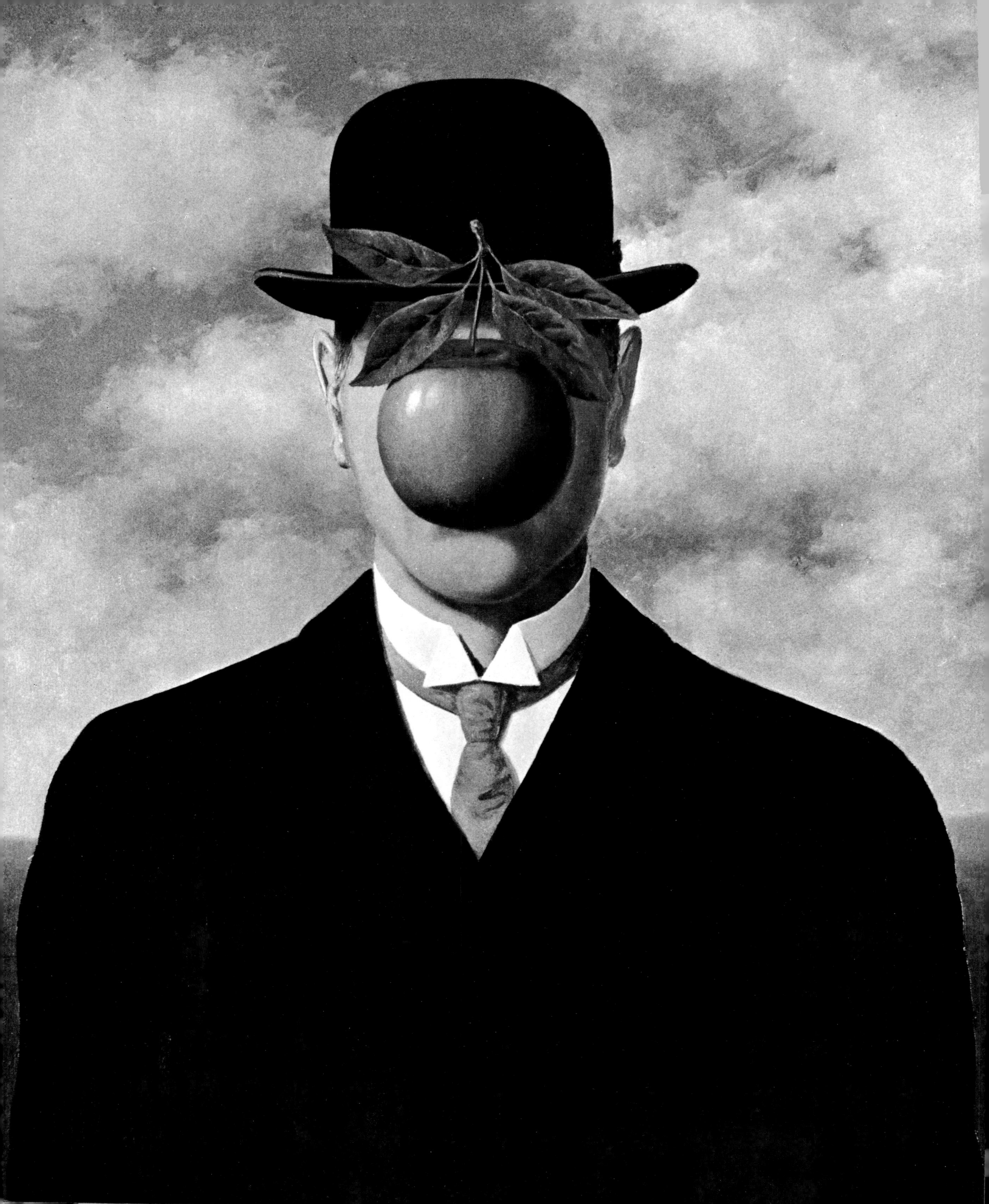

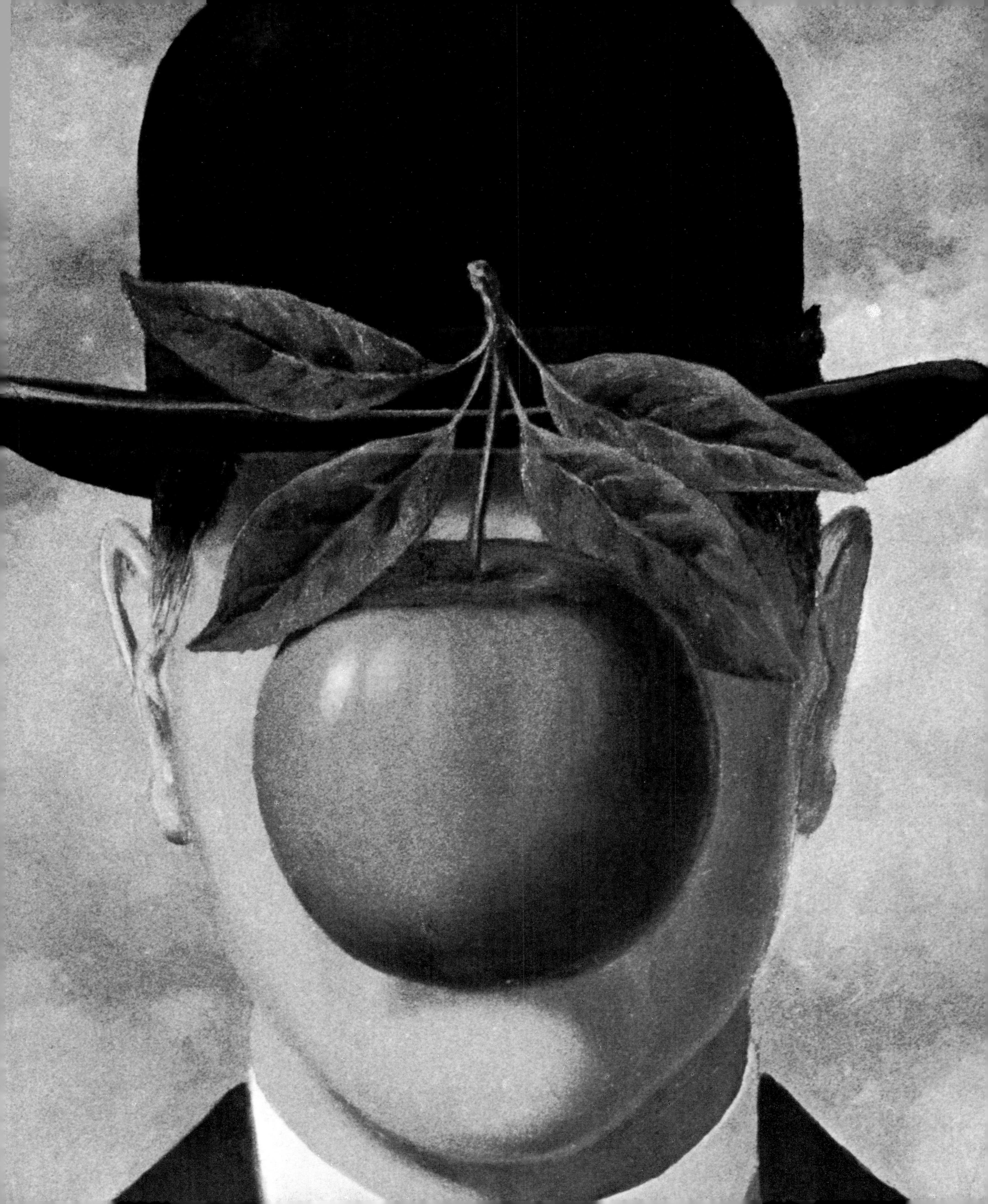

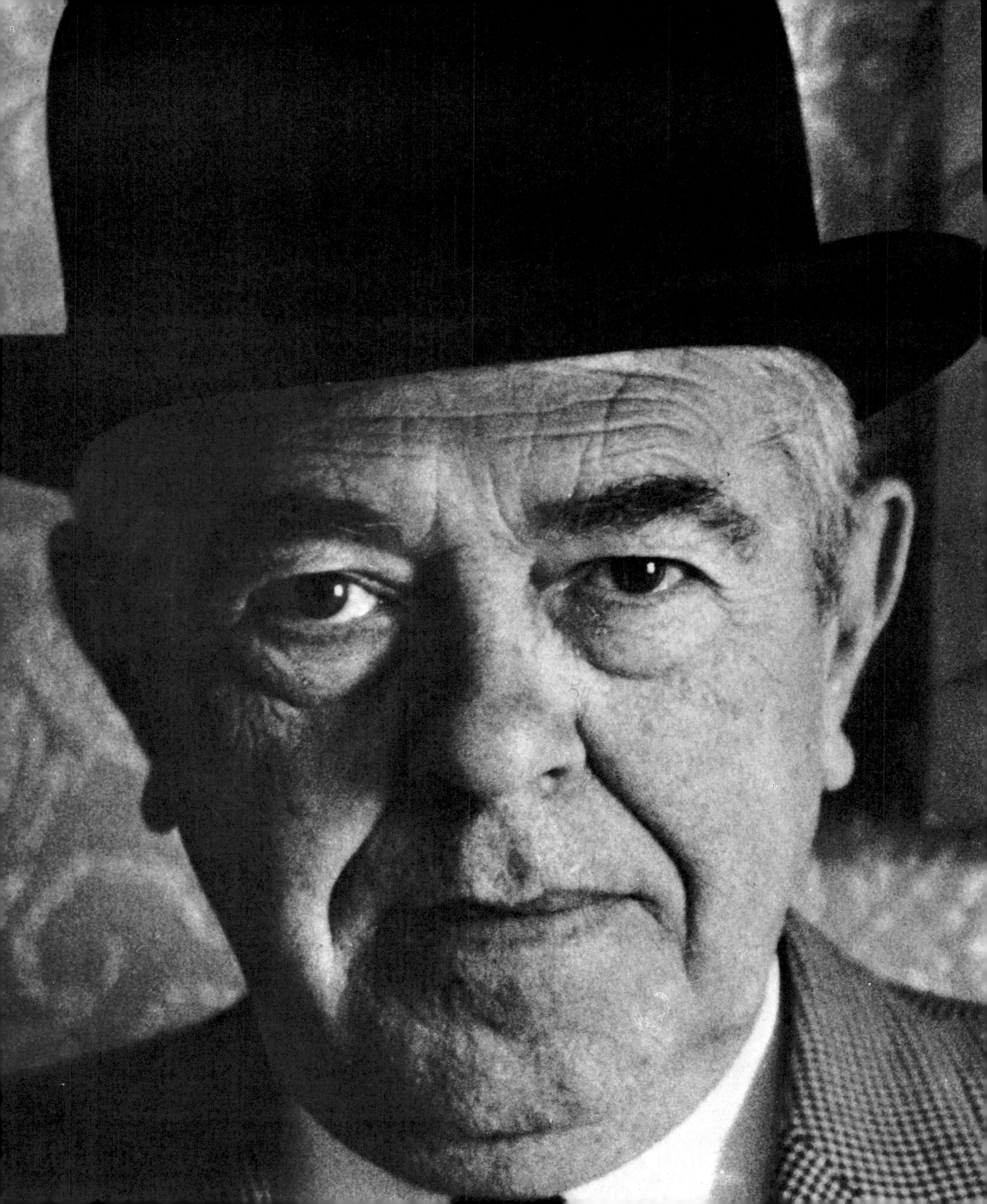

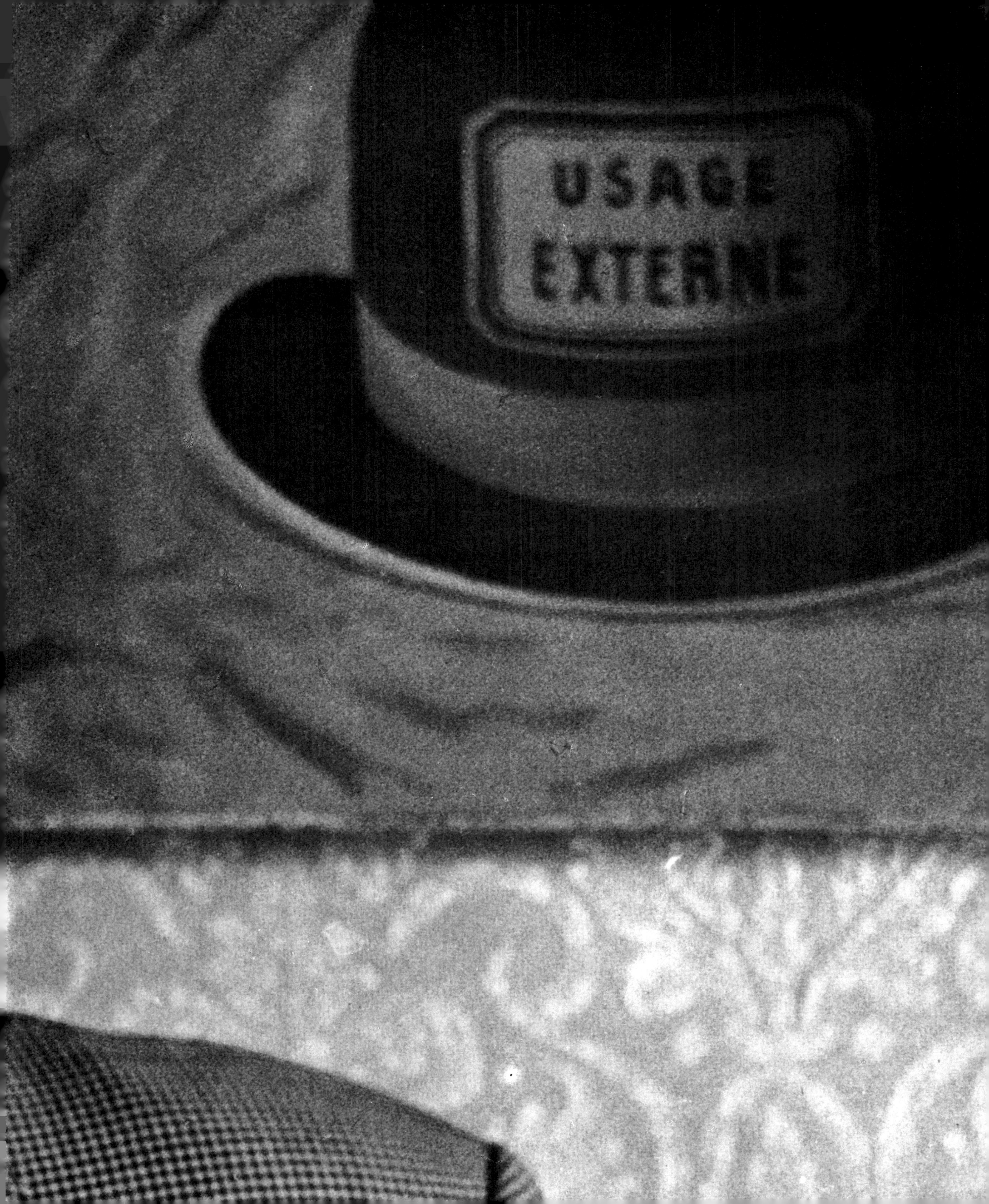
USAGE
EXTERNE

Art Director : Jean Saucet.
Text by René Passeron.
Translated from the French by Elisabeth Abbot.
Library of Congress Catalog Card Number : 72-189278.
I.S.B.N. Hardcover : 2-85018-098-X
Softcover : 2-85018-099-8.

Great Journies
1926 / 25.6 × 59

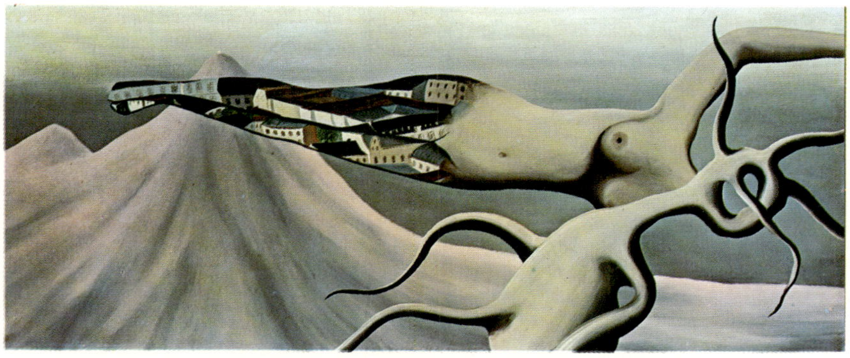

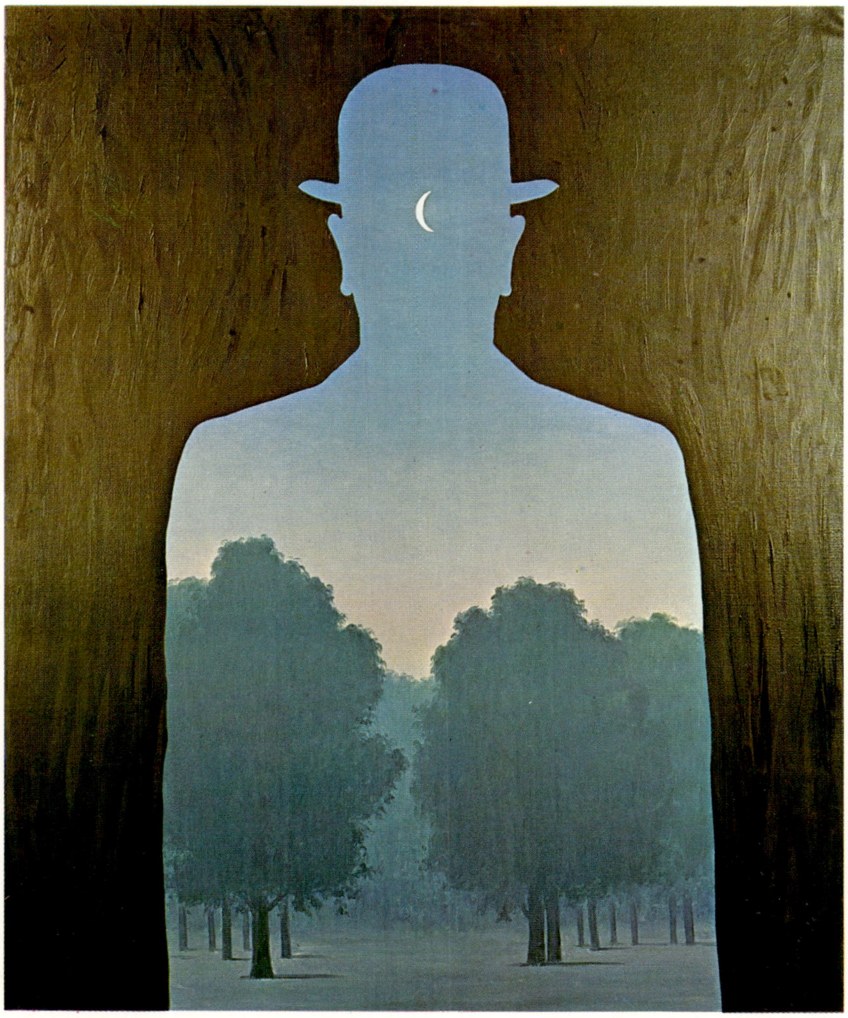

The Friend of Order
1964 / 39 × 31.9

Opposite page:
Popular Panorama
1926 / 47.5 × 31.5

1947 / 23.6 × 16.5

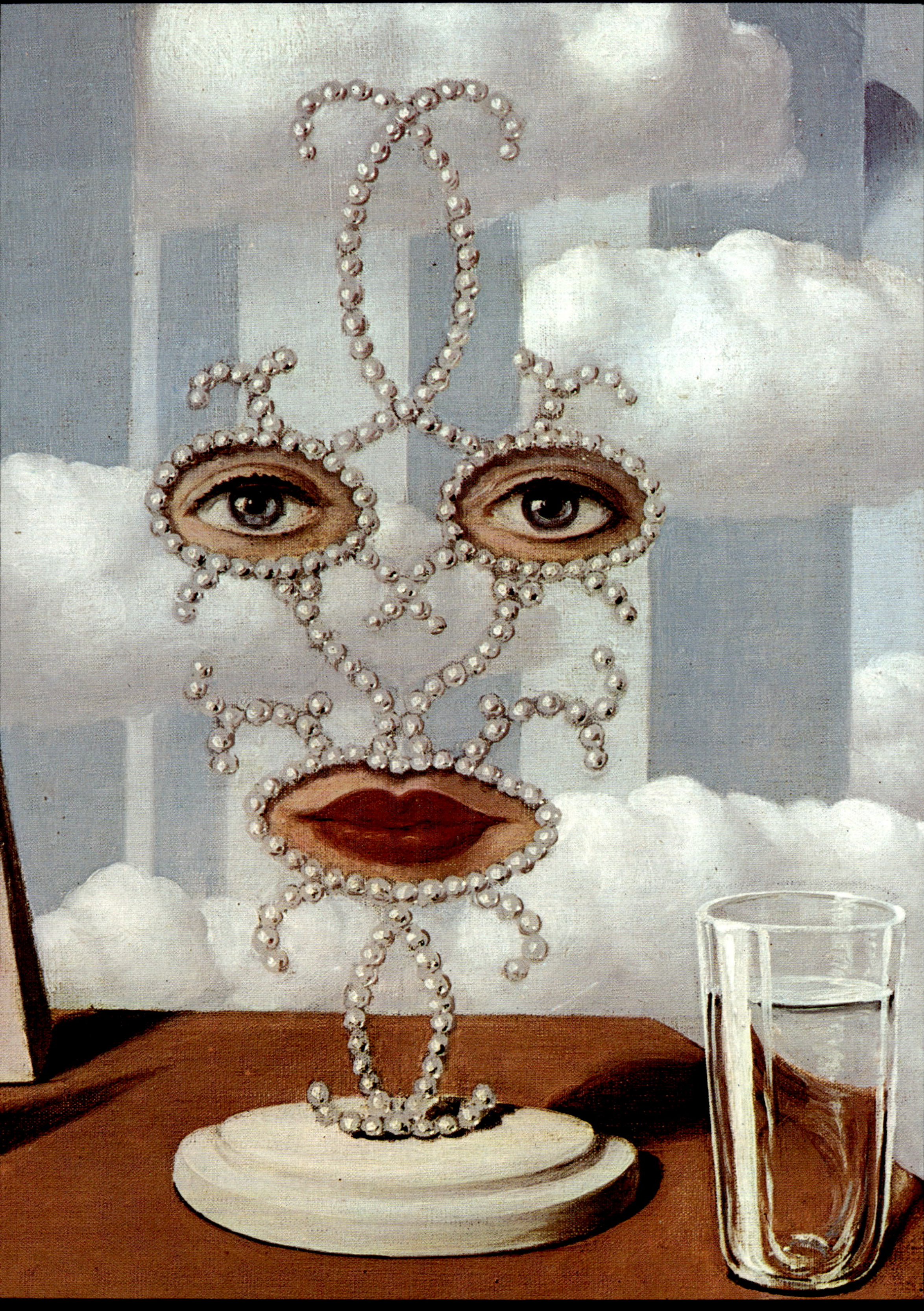

2. THE INNER NIGHT

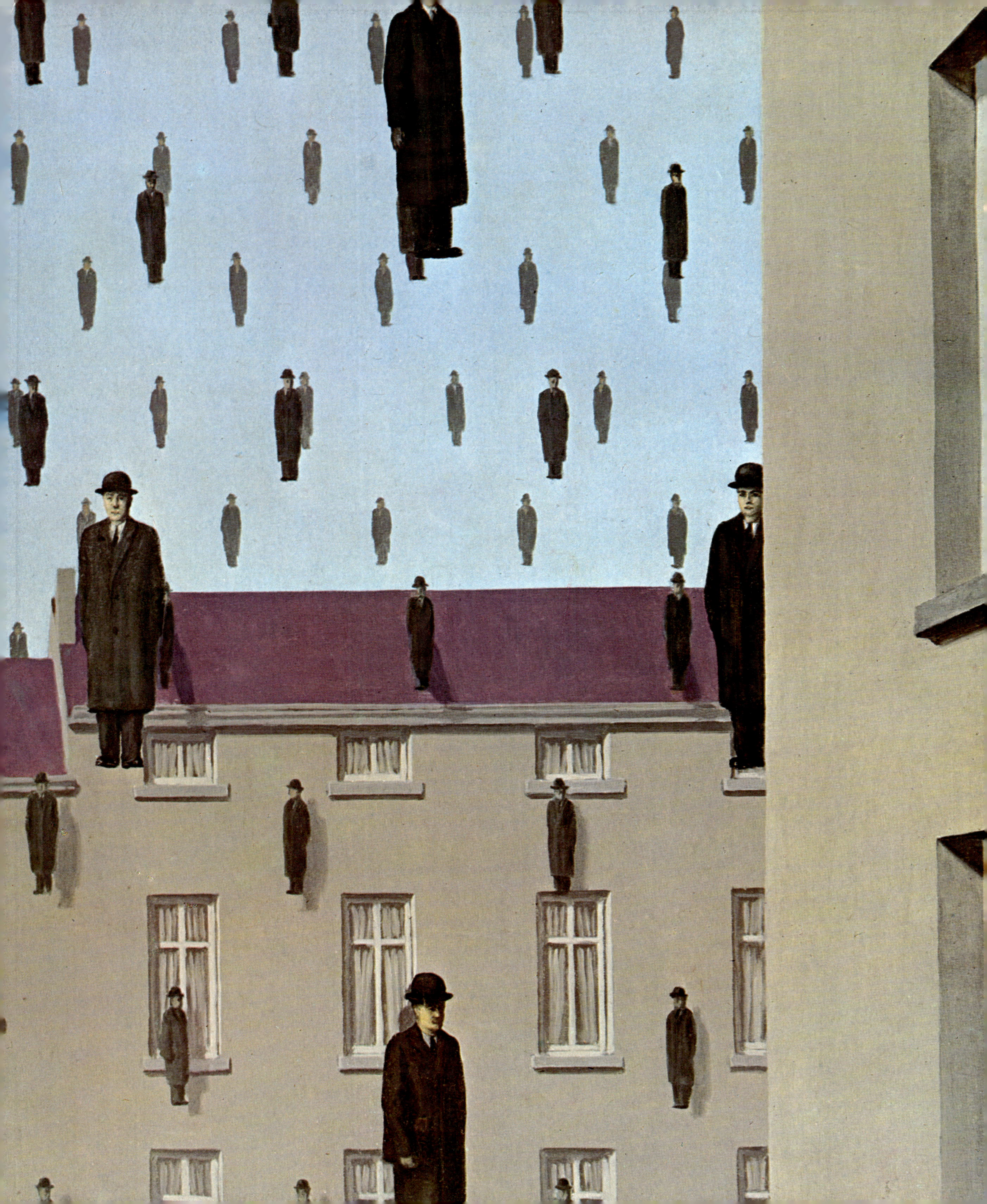

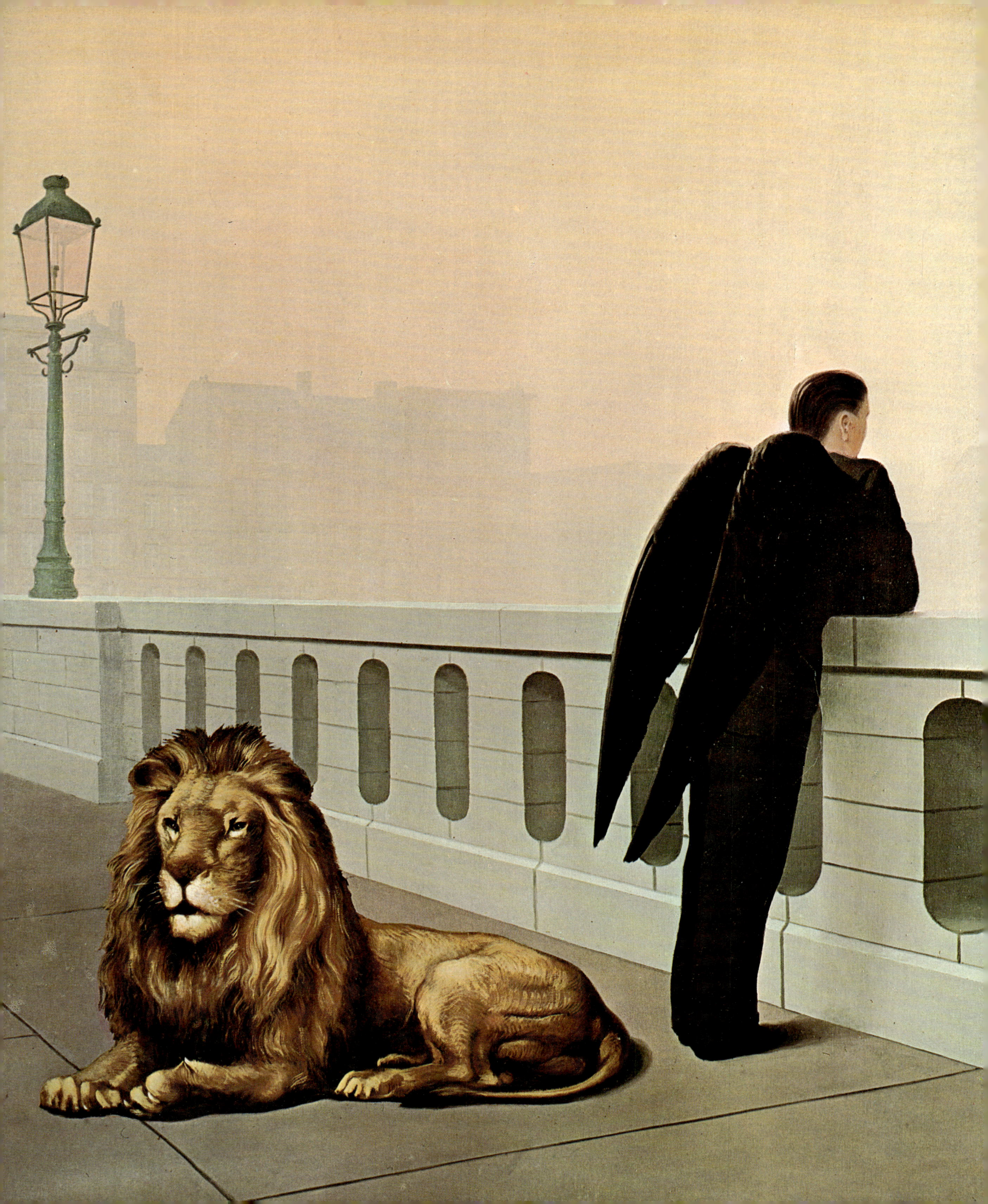

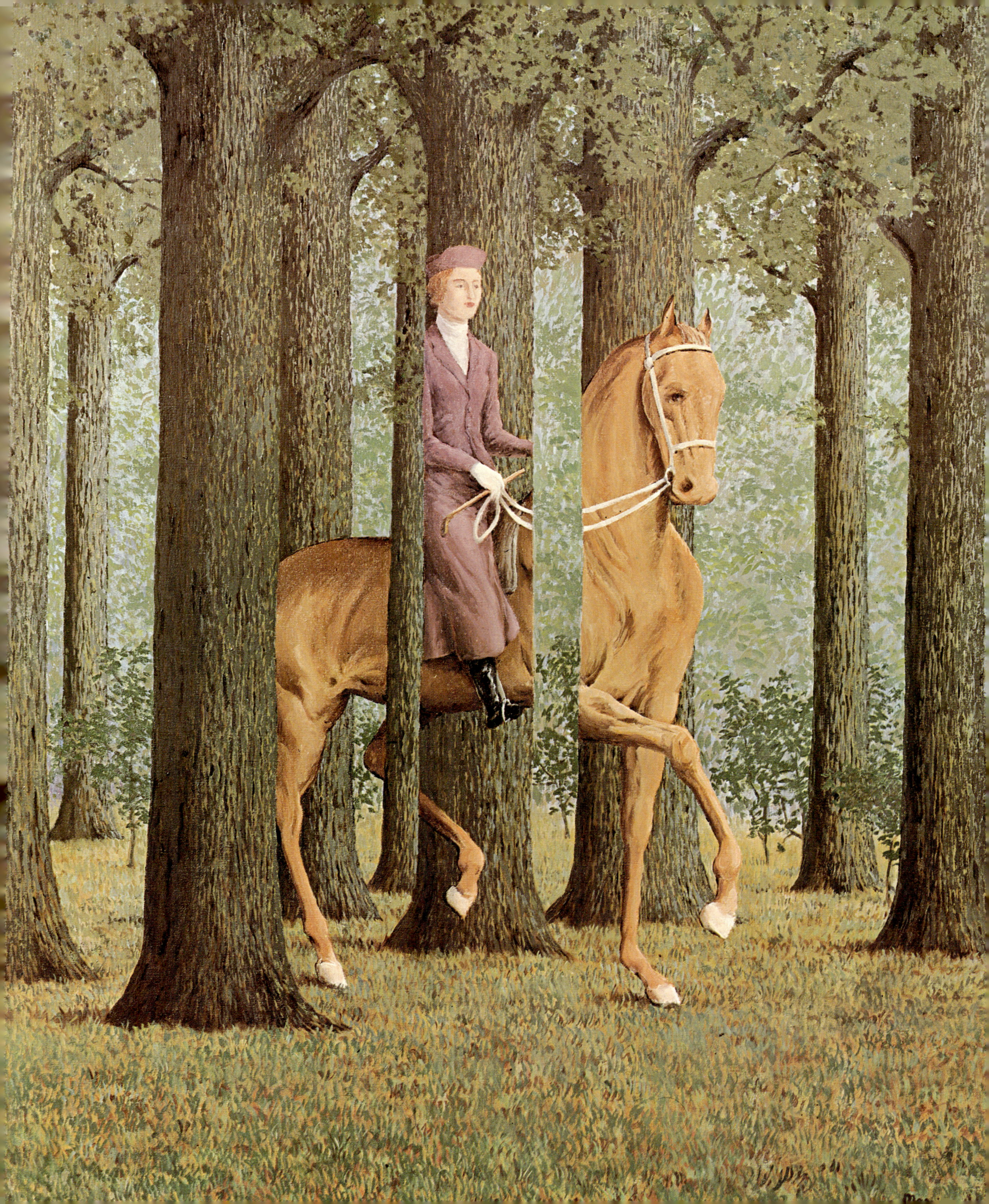

LISTENING TO GEORGETTE MAGRITTE

How did you happen to meet René Magritte?

At Charleroi, where I lived as a child, the annual fair was in progress. There was a carrousel on the square of the upper town. "Come and have a ride on the mill," a very young man said to me. After that René and I met almost daily on our way to school. Then came the war of 1914... René left for Brussels and I lost sight of him. After the armistice, for family reasons, I followed my sister Léontine to Brussels where we were employed in a shop that sold painter's supplies. One day after lunch in the spring of 1920, I was walking with my sister in the botanical garden when I ran into René. He was delighted to see me! And from that day we were never separated... After he finished his military service we were married.

Things that happen in childhood often have a lasting influence. Did Magritte ever speak to you of his?

René never spoke of his mother; he never confided anything about his relatives to me. Neither the past nor the future interested him, only the present. He did not have a family feeling and he loved only his wife, his Pomeranian dog, his "home," to the exclusion of everything else. "When I travel," he said, "the best moment is when I come home." He did not like automobiles and he had owned only one – for five days. He preferred to receive his friends rather than to go to them. Sometimes he would keep them till morning – if the conversation interested him; if not, he tired quickly. He abhorred banalities, the commonplaces of everyday life... Money problems did not interest him. Sometimes he confessed to his friends that he was bored. But that, I do not believe; if he wasn't painting, he was playing chess or solving chess problems. Chess took up many hours of his life. Sometimes he would ask me: "Play one of Satie's *gymnopédie* for me," for he was very fond of Satie, Debussy, Ravel. "In music," he would say, "I go no further than Debussy and Ravel." He did not talk much. Neither gay nor sad one had the impression that he was always reflecting. He was a cerebral, of a rather restless temperament. He read a great deal.

What books did he read?

Though he liked Marcel Aymé and detective stories... he also delved into the philosophers, especially Heidegger, Hegel, Kant and also the poets. He read an re-read Edgar Allan Poe's *Tales of the Grotesque and Arabesque*.

Can you tell me what his convictions were?

As a small boy he used to tease the maid-servant, Anaïs, by making the sign of the cross at table or by setting up altars in his bedroom... Child's play! He never went to mass. Was he a believer? I hardly think so. He thought there was a mystery in the world. When he was talking with Paul Collinet I often heard him say : "There is a mystery in the universe, but what is it?"

Where, in your opinion, does his real "departure" lie?

All his life René never willingly visited the exhibitions of other painters, no more than he would put foot in a museum. In Florence he went to the Uffizi. Fifteen minutes later he came out: he had seen what he wanted to see – the Botticelli. In his youth he told me, he had been greatly impressed by Chirico's *Chant d'Amour,* so much so in fact that tears came to his eyes. His real "departure" was the *Jockey perdu*. But before he finished that picture, he had painted another which showed an arm reaching out through an open window to catch a bird. That canvas made a great impression on me. And René was aware of it.

What suggested the subject of the *Jockey perdu* to him?

My husband talked about "inspired thought," in other words, inspiration, an inspiration not aroused by an exterior fact, but that suddenly came to his mind.

How did he get his ideas for a picture?

For example, he wanted to paint a piano (he painted only familiar objects), and in doing that he wanted to create a poetic image, not an unimportant image. He searched, reflected, made sketches starting with the basic object: piano, leaf, bird... forcing himself to find other elements that could give him a poetic value. That is what he did for *la Page blanche* in which leaves are shown against the background of a nocturnal sky, with a moon plastered on the leaves. He had wanted to show a moon placed in front of the leaves, but without hiding the moon. Because he claimed that visible objects never become invisible and that a letter in an envelope was not, for that reason, invisible. But to come back to our picture. At first he had painted a crescent moon to avoid confusion with the representation of the sun. But that crescent looked as though it were behind the foliage... Then he painted a full moon.

What objects did he prefer?

Cup-and-ball, curtains, tinkling harness bells...

Is that small bell one finds in so many of his canvasses a symbol?

There is never any symbol in his canvasses. He would have been furious if anyone had told him he was painting symbols. He always said one could not paint a feeling, a notion, an idea... René started from an object, a figure, a mountain... Never from an idea.

Did Magritte paint from models?

There were never any cup-and-balls or bells in our house... René painted from his imagination. Except for the nudes. And then I was his model even when he was not painting body details... If we happened to be in the country, he would curve his fingers around his eye like a monocle the better to see the countryside or else he would gaze attentively at a stone, a leaf... But he never brought anything back, he never sketched from nature.

How did he get his titles?

The titles always came after the picture. Sometimes friends suggested a title and René would consider whether to accept it or not. That, among others, was the way Nougé found *la Mémoire*. Scutenaire and Collinet also found quite a few; sometimes they tried out several... The title is not an explanation of the painting. It is a poetic element that is part of the picture. This proves that Magritte never began with an idea.

And what of death?

"Let us not talk of that...," he used to say to me...

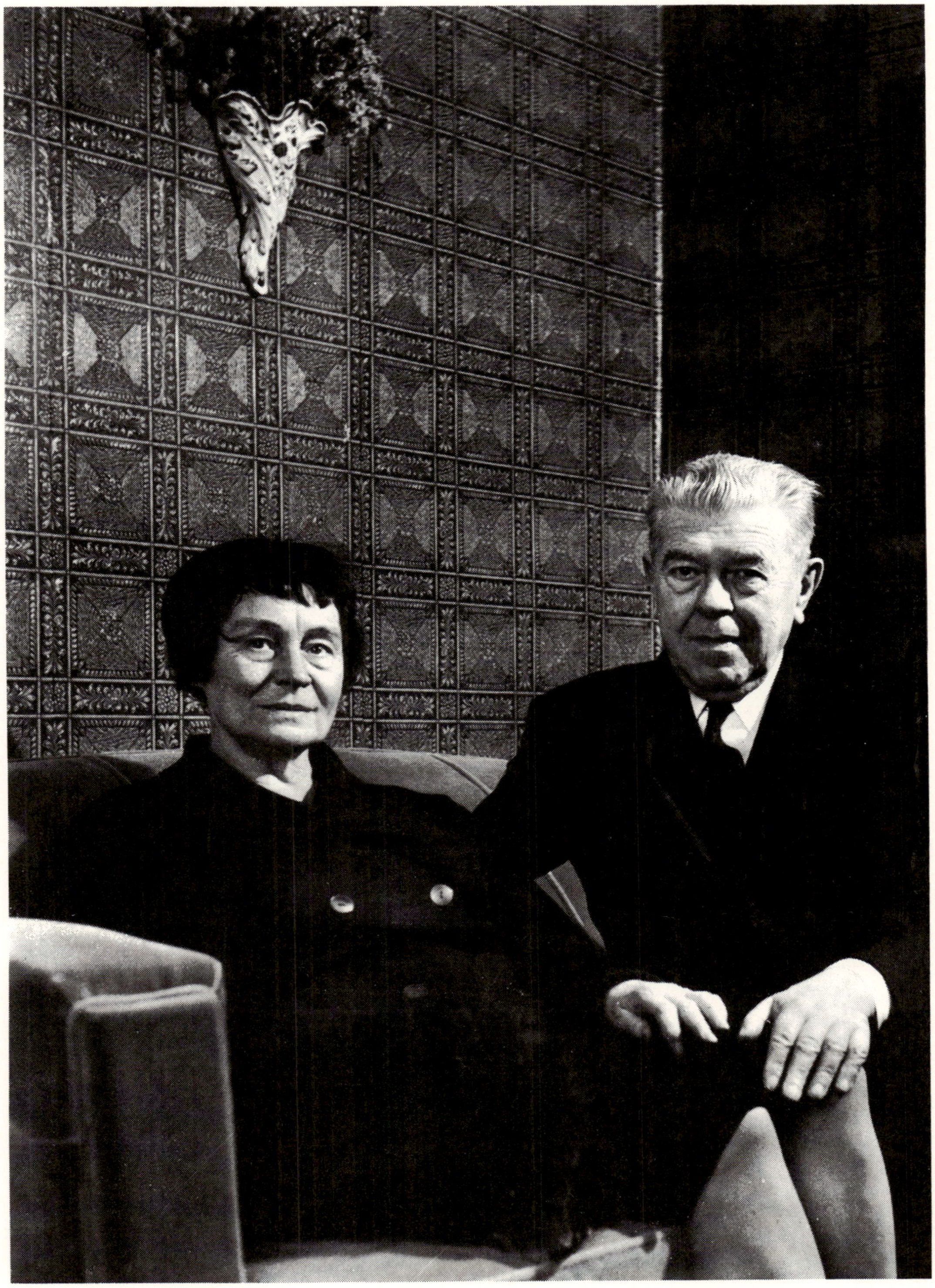

1967 / 15 × 18.1

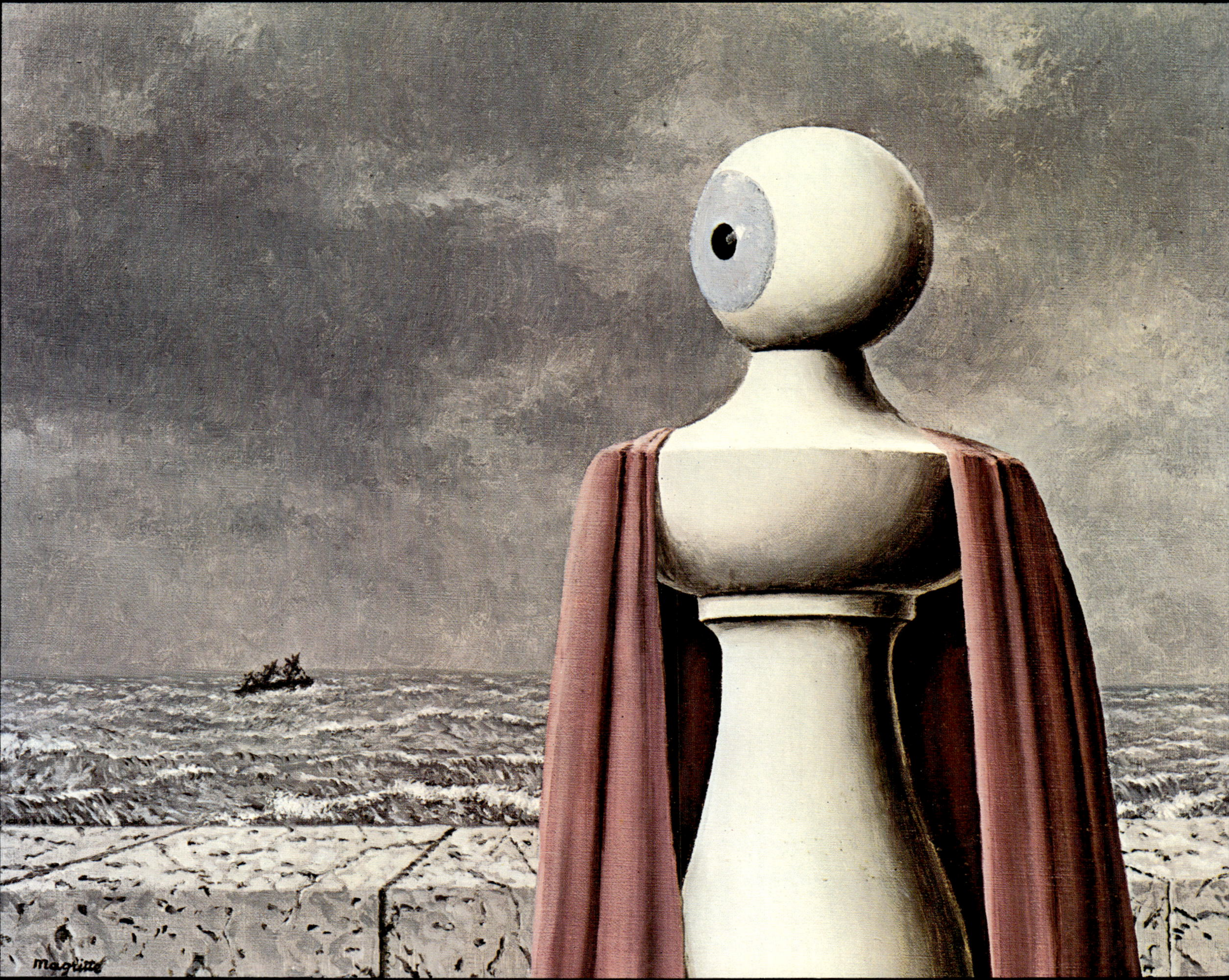

1. THE GREAT COLD SPACES

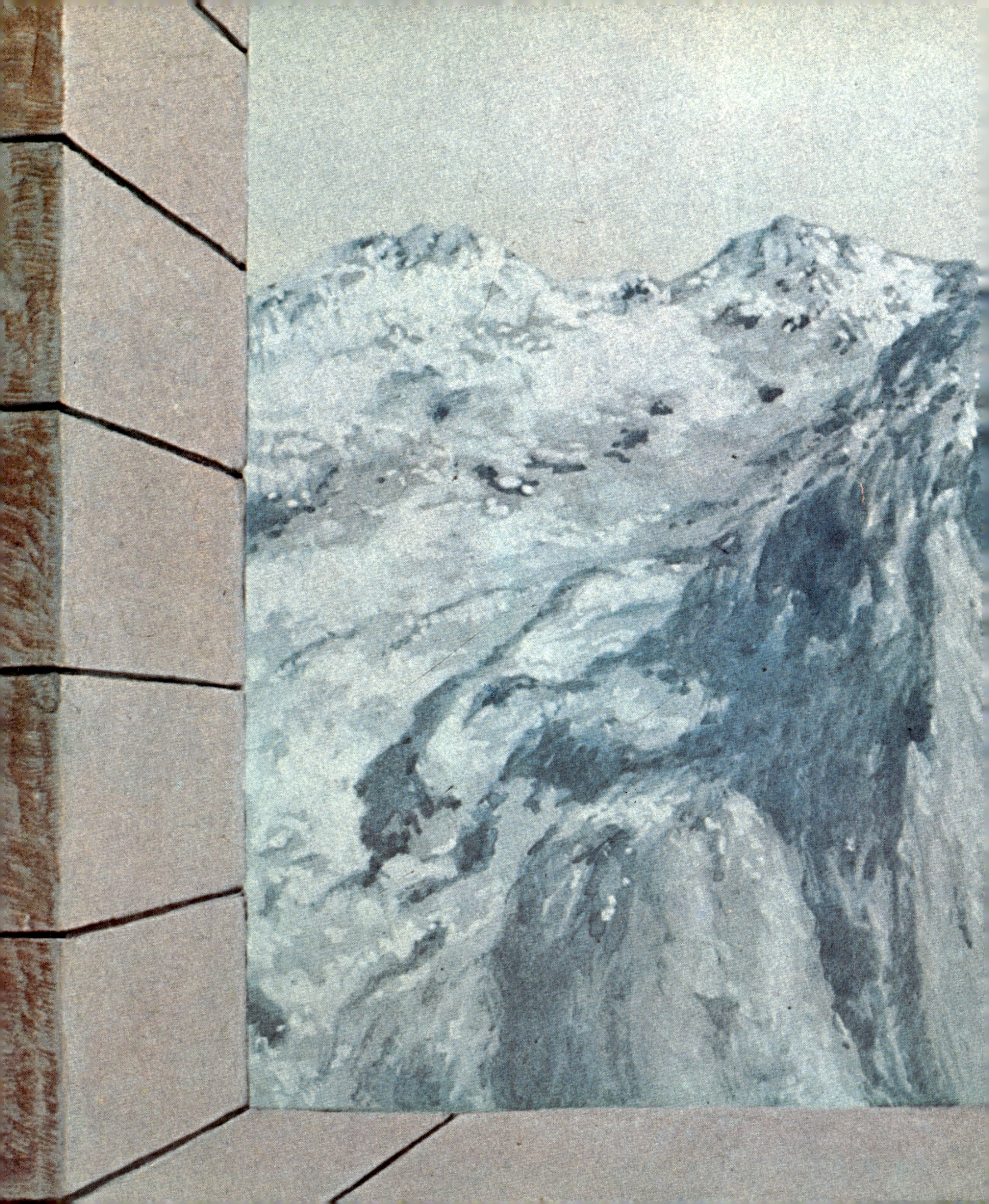

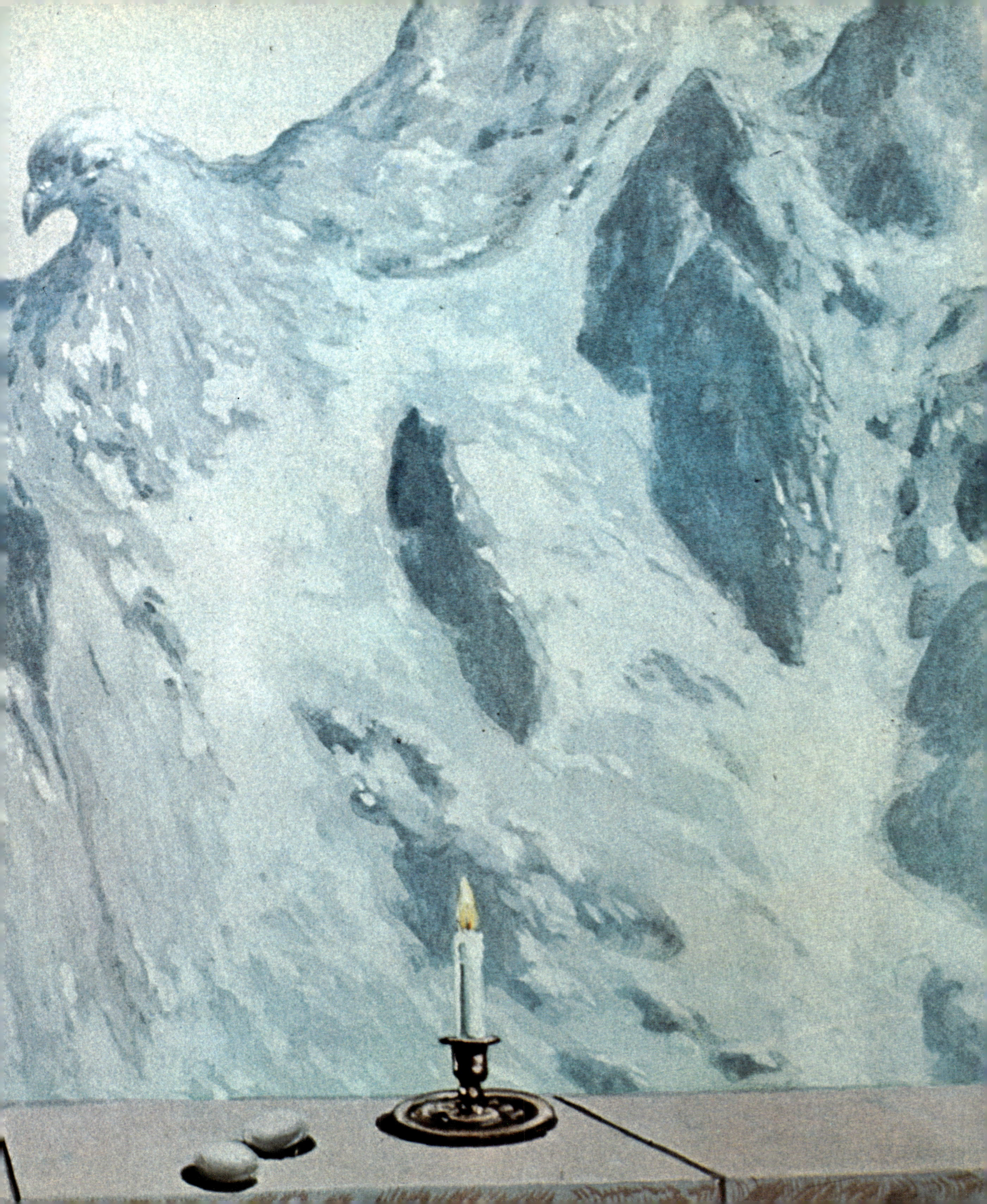

On the preceding pages:
The Domain of Arnheim
Gouache 1950 / 13.4 × 18.1

Below:
The Fair Captive
Gouache 1956 / 15.3 × 17.8

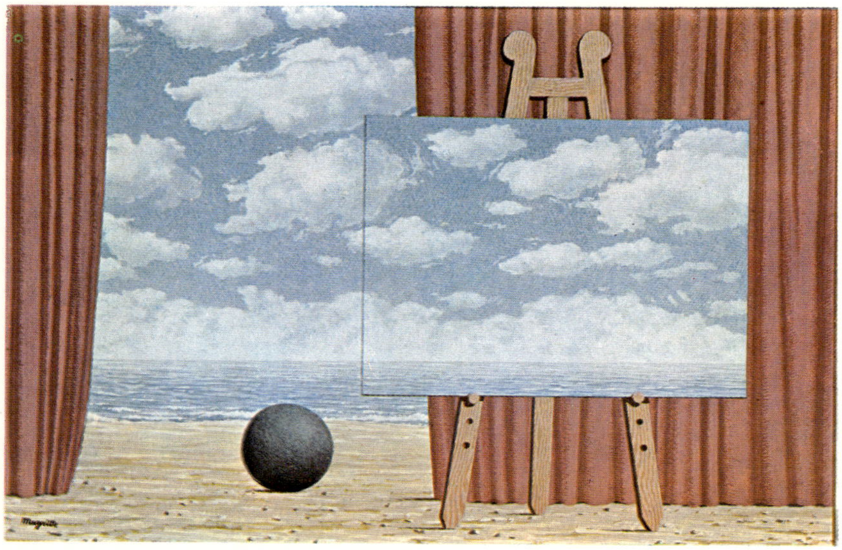

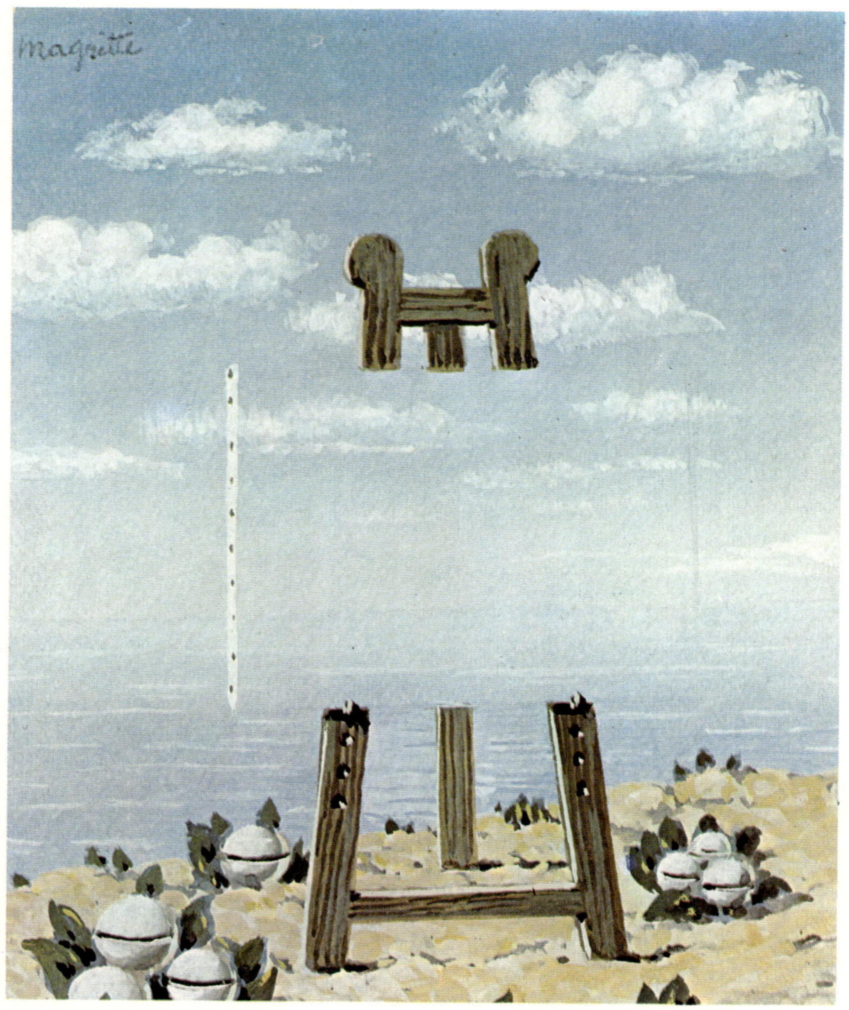

The Human Condition
Gouache 1948 / 7.1 × 6.3

Opposite page:
The Large Family
1947 / 39.4 × 31.9

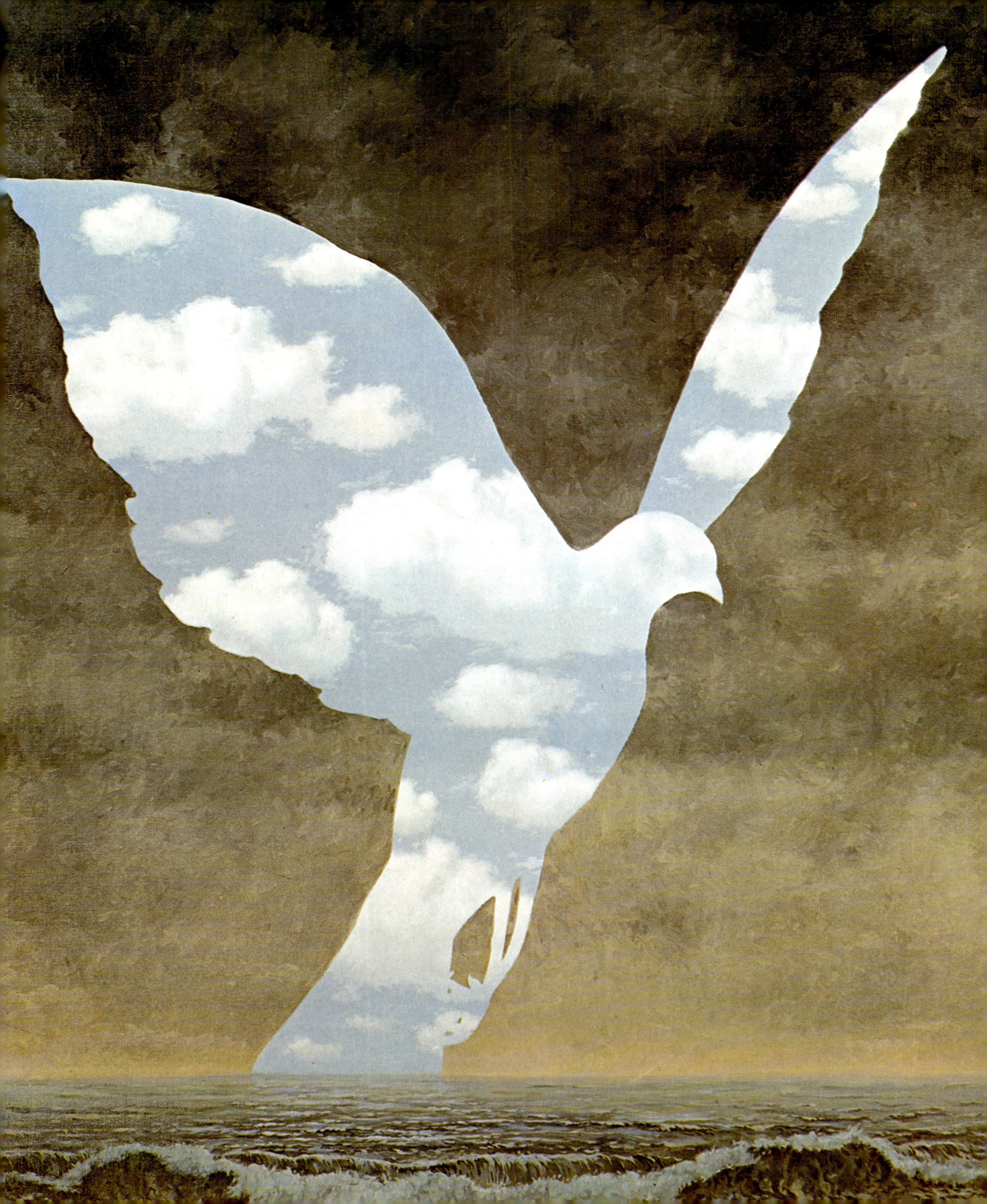

Fashionable People
1950 / 16.1 × 13.4

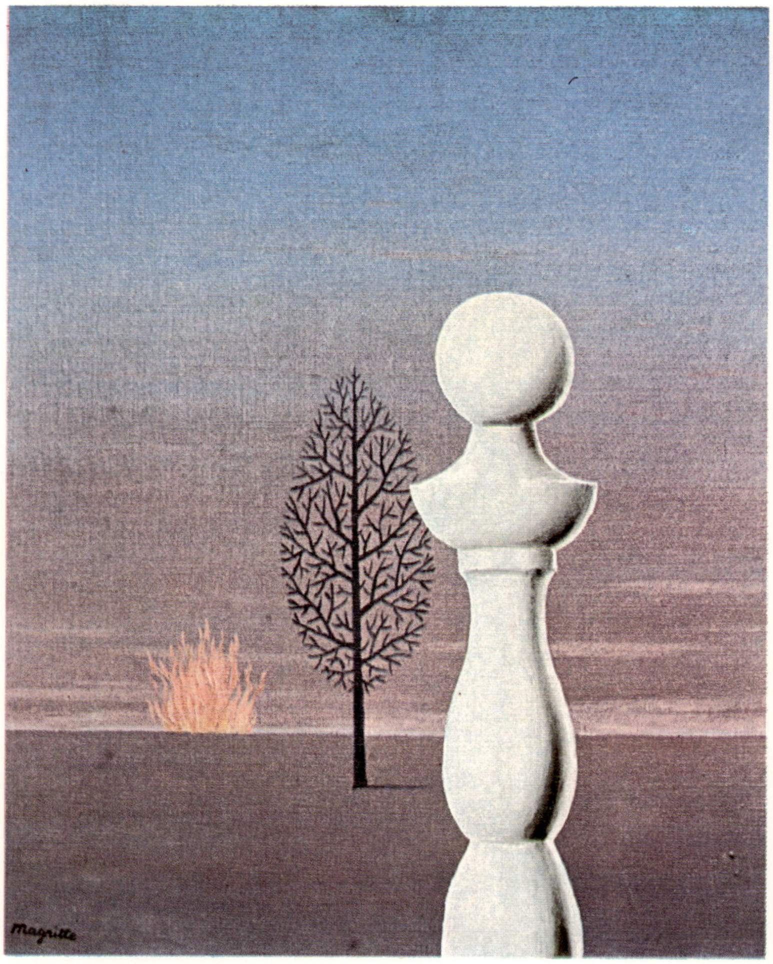

The Lost Jockey
Gouache 1942 / 19.8 × 33.1

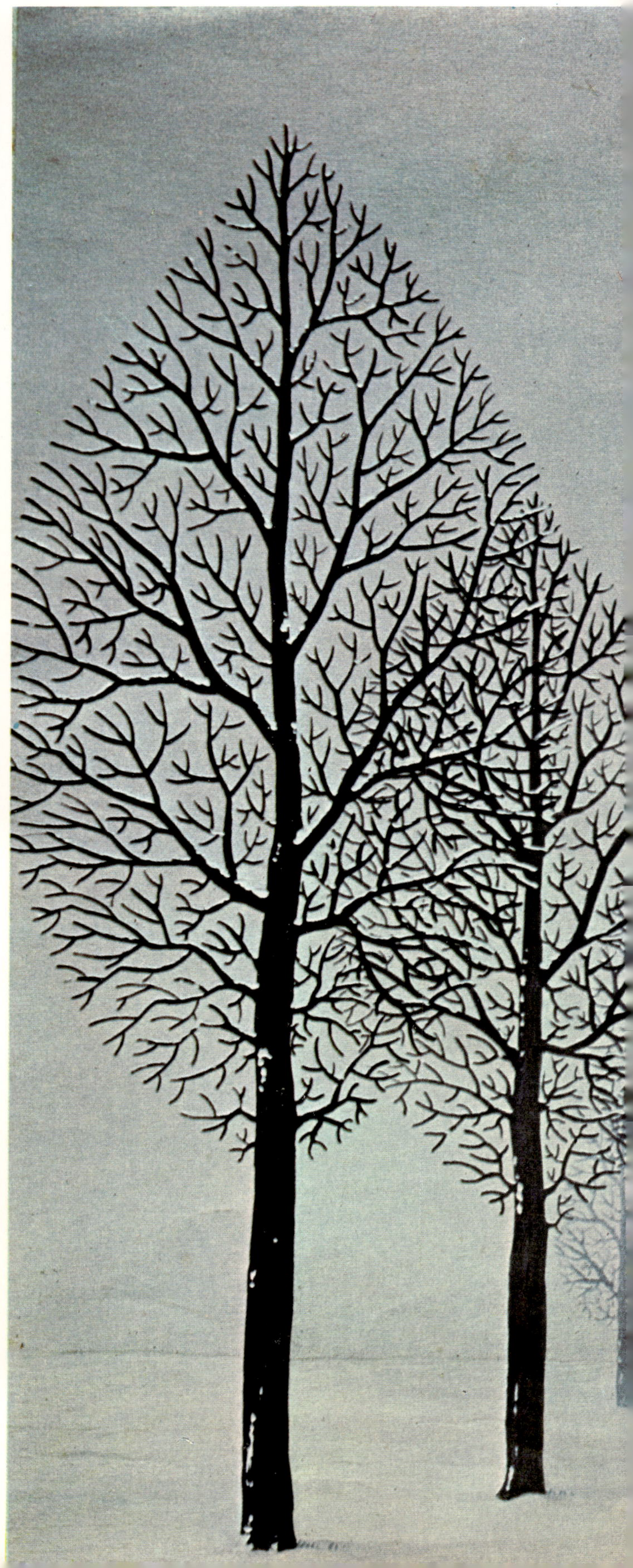

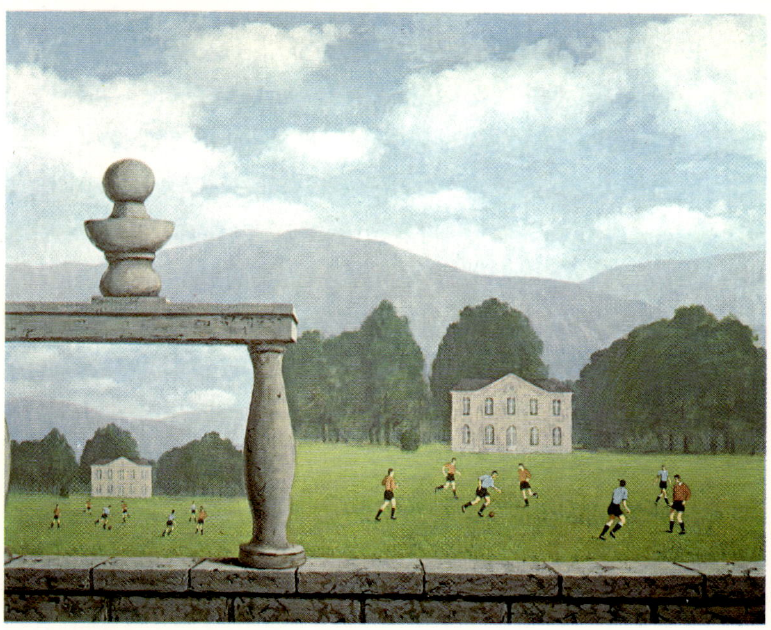

Representation
1962 / 31.5 × 39

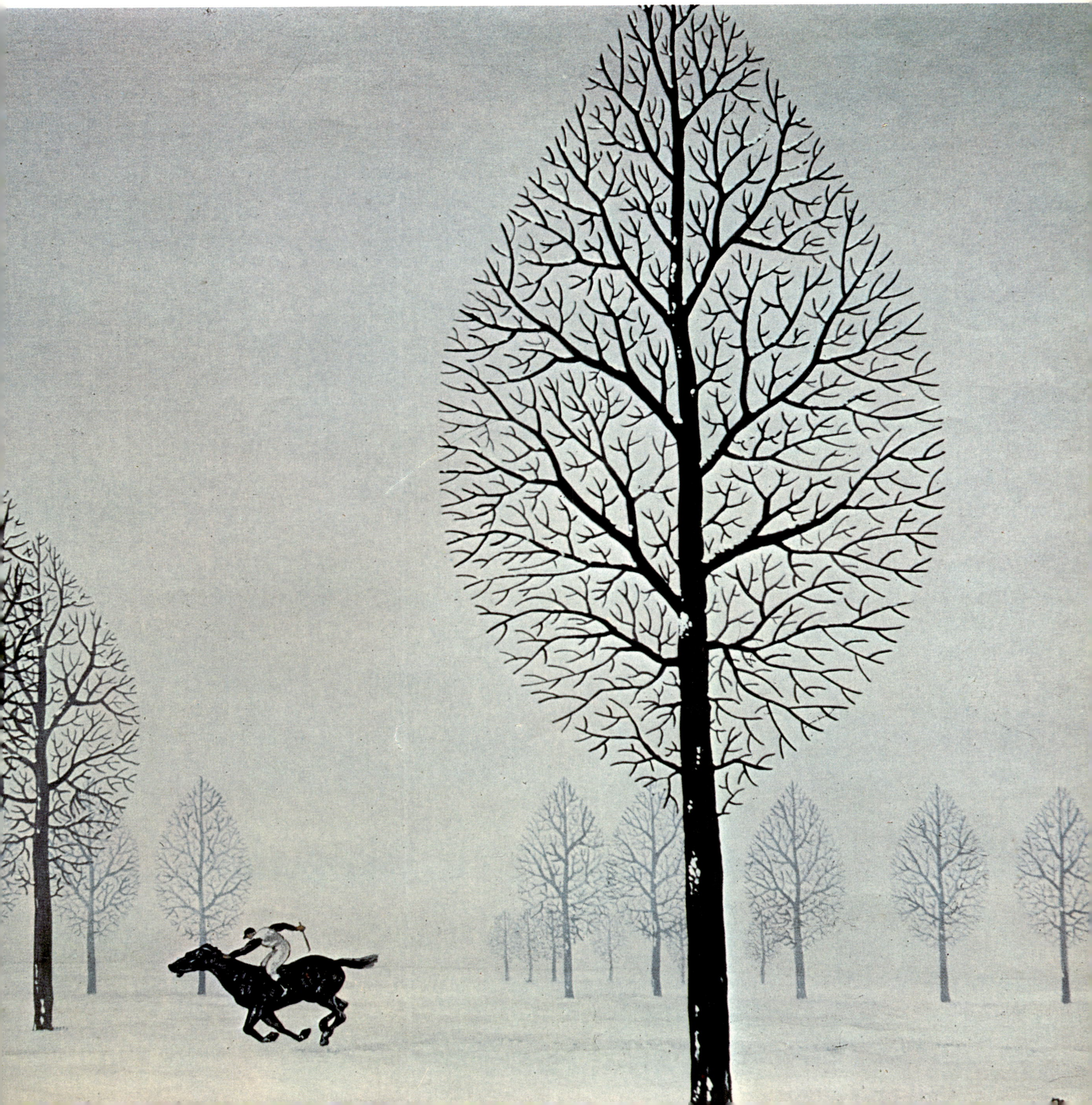

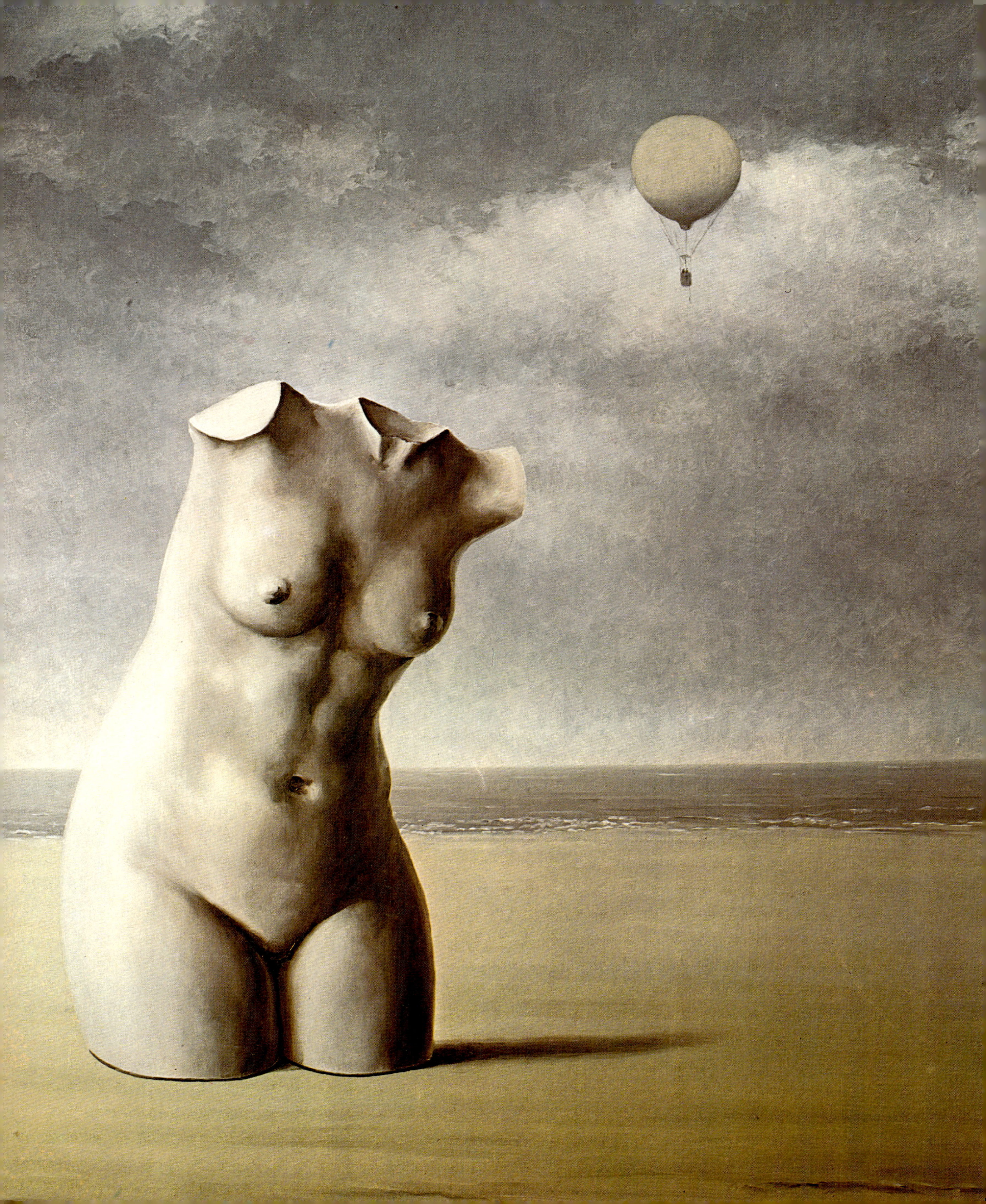

Victory
1939 / 28.8 × 20.5

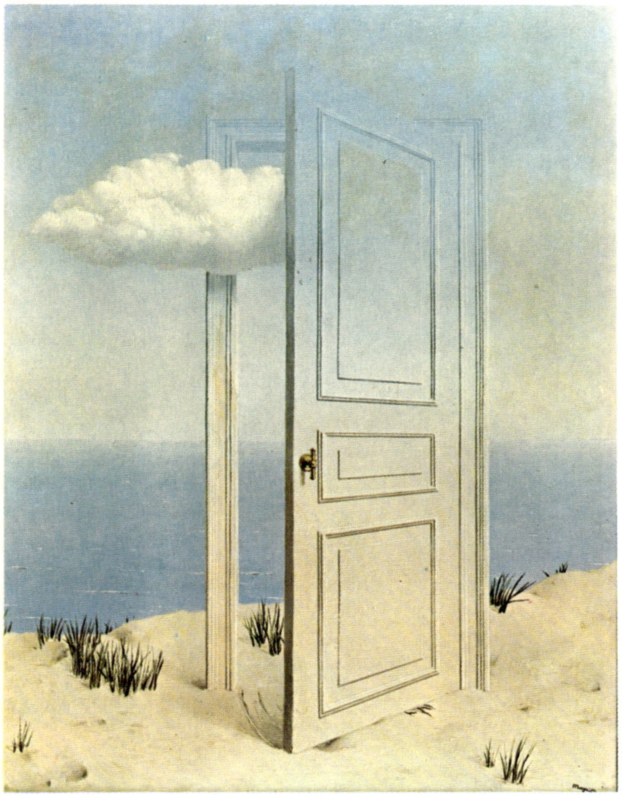

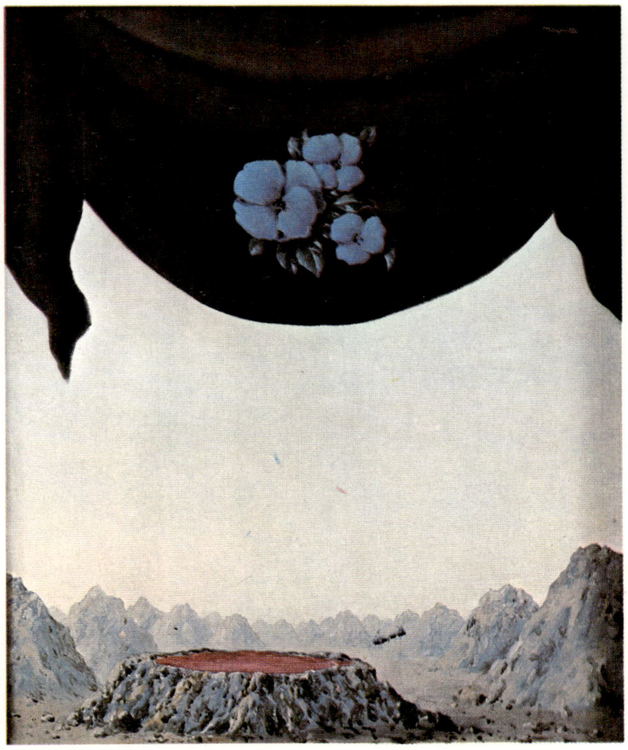

The Palace of Memories
1939 / 18.5 × 15

Opposite page:
When the Hour will Strike
1946 / 39.4 × 31.9

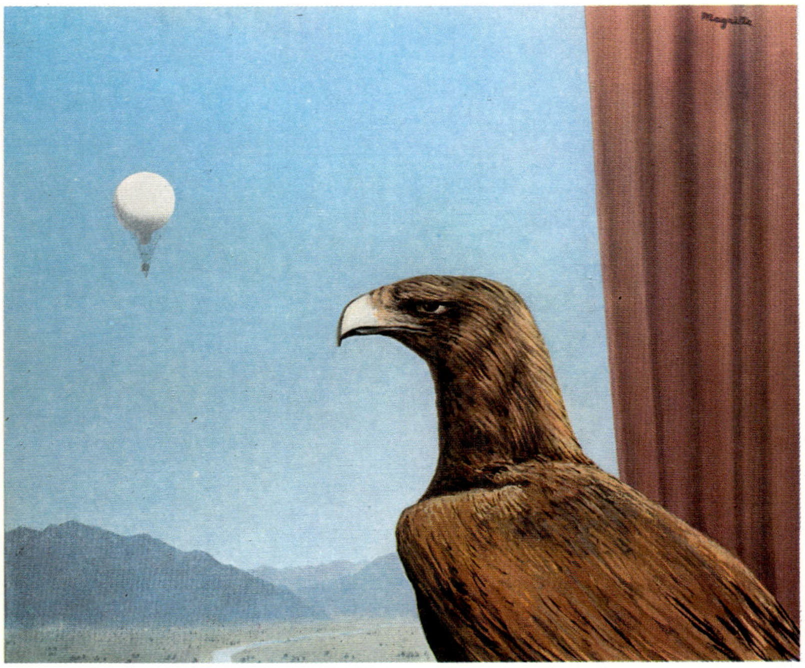

The Thief
1967 / 17.3 × 19.8

On the following pages:
The World Awakened (detail)
1958 / 15.8 × 19.8

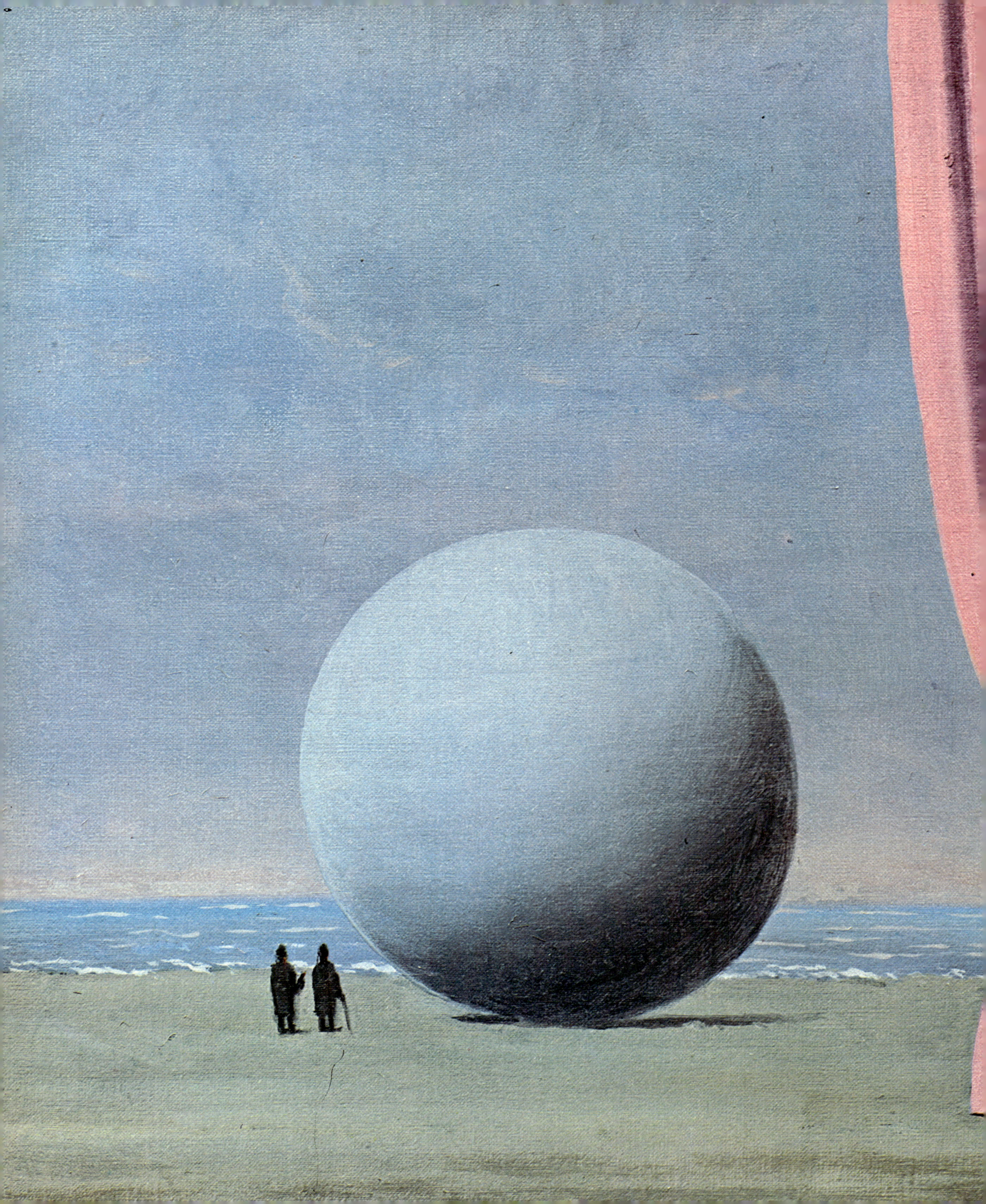

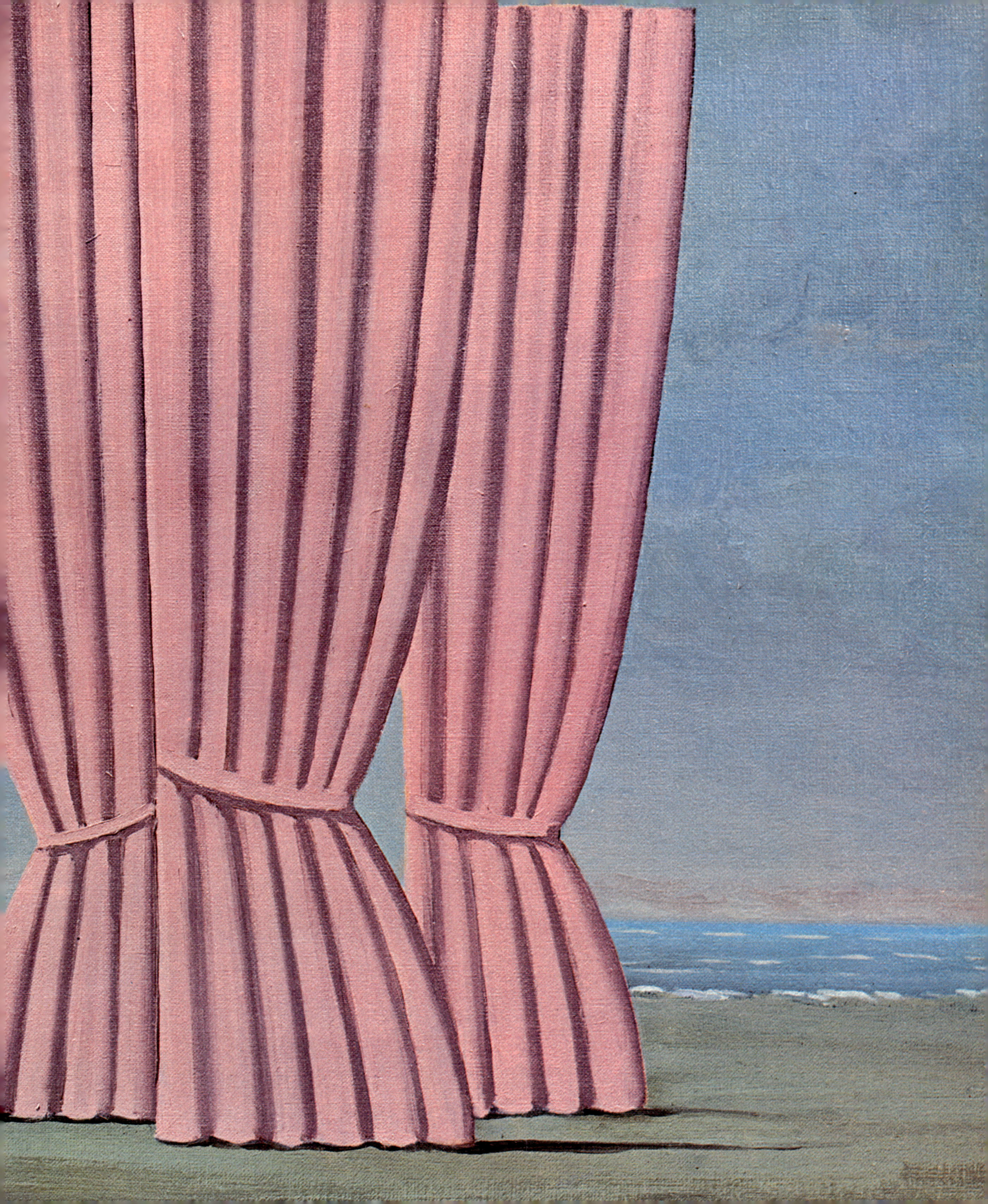

1 THE GREAT COLD SPACES

Then images rush forward and are lost, they rise up and crash down again at their same height. Then realism and unreality are needed.
Gaston Bachelard: *l'Air et les Songes,* Paris, Corti, 1943, p. 13.

With René Magritte we enter the universe of cold. No lace-like hoar frost, no icicles. Forms are frozen without flourishes. The baroque geometry of snow crystals is foreign to him. Magritte looks upward. The slope of the glacier becomes rocky at the crest and there is an eagle's head, his back, his eye. The transparency of the petrified sky shrouds the immobility of that rapacious profile. Magritte's outer space would have led Bachelard (if he had sought other than literary examples in *l'Air et les Songes*) to place this painter not far from Nietzsche among the poets of the great icy space. He was different, however, from the philosopher in the ease with which he moved in that air: whereas one man breathes painfully on the heights, the other soars there with the somewhat vague smile of an ironical man. Like the man with black wings leaning over the parapet, he raises his eyes, but he looks down from on high.
In one of Magritte's variants, the *Jockey perdu* races between trees that are bare of leaves. In his silhouette is concentrated all the wildness of that gallop — what panic carries him away? — skimming the ground at the bottom of the picture, while the great trees, denuded but leaf-shaped, are spread about on all sides, immobile against the boundless sky. The essential object is therefore farthest off: the nine-pin upright on the plain, the lighted candle in front of the mountain of ice, the white cloth on the easel to reduce to nothing the point of a perspective, and even the immense bird, the astonishing dove that emerges from the sea like the stump of antique woman and the fire-balloon that flies away or the little men who make speeches about the non-meaning of a sphere set there in all its enormity, all those things most singled out by the poets of painting are merely notes picked out in a webless sky. Not symbols if we are to believe the painter: "A person would have to know nothing about my painting to associate it with a naïve or a scholarly symbol," he wrote (1). For the invisible is not a problem to Magritte, nor are even the signs he had to invent to translate it. The visible, he adds, "is rich enough to form a poetic language evocative of the mystery of the invisible and of the visible." No doubt. And the visible is not the real, for it is already the sensitive translation of reality. That Magritte gave the title *la Condition humaine* to that famous painting in which we see a canvas on its easel placed side by side with the landscape it is supposed to represent so that nature and painting become one, proves the keenness of his meditation on the mystery of the visible. We never see things as they actually are and the artist never depicts them as he sees them; absurd therefore to think you are painting reality.
In this respect nothing could be less realistic than the art of Magritte. But neither is he one to be diverted from the triviality of pipes and bottles to make of painting a pure music of forms. Between the abstract which scorns to portray objects and realism which delights in it, Magritte boldly slips his cold humor, his serious player, in a representation to ridicule all representations. As the heir of Dada, his surrealist musing is centered on the ambiguity of the visible. Instead of being liberated by the marvelous, it deepens our concern at being in the world. And rightly, the visible hides some of the visible; there is no limit. Every hidden object may at some time become visible. Beyond what we actually see there is a potential visible: which is what our eyes desire because they do not have it — the Beyond of our retinal perspective at every moment. And it is right that it be available to our pictorial double-view. Space is therefore filled with objects. Through them connections are established and a construction arises, often absurd, but always frank, open. Space is a real Beyond, a glacial beyond whose cold falls down again on the motionlessness of objects. Are they able to move? Now and then the wind blows in a door, set in the midst of a dune over which a cloud passes or else the same wind churns the waves of the sea against the spectator's legs, birds fly (whether they be of clay or of rocks), the horsewoman rides her horse calmly through the woods. This is unusual. Immobility is part of the mystery of things. Are nine-pins made to stand upright? Magritte does not knock over a single one. The apple does not fall; it stays on a level with the face, the countenance at once derisory and sinister, of a well-dressed man wearing a bowler hat. Behind the man with black wings the lion is as rooted to the spot as the gas-jet. Naked women (except in Magritte's impressionist period, 1940-1948) are painted as cold as marble and they do not make any gestures. Worse than that, here is Madame Récamier caught in the mold of her coffin, like the people in Manet's balcony. Is there a more definitive stiffness than that of those coffins that take the form of the living man who, for that matter, never moved when he let himself be taken? Or else clay petrifies all... No, with Magritte, it is the "spectator" who moves, who travels, seeking a way to withdraw from what Hogarth called "perspective made to look ridiculous" and quickly lost in the inner contradictions of that space which at first sight looks innocent, but which soon moves one to anguish. To our eyes even the infinite is a comfort. With Magritte the infinite runs wild.
Here is *Golconde*. Against a background of commonplace façades and sky, an airy crowd of men in bowlers. Wearing long coats, they stand legs together, perfectly motionless. Some of them are close to us, others far away, but all of them are in front of the house. The depth of the sky therefore covers the whole picture in spite

(1) In the catalogue: "Magritte, le sens propre," Paris, Iolas, 1964.

of the proximity of this façade. The latter, filled with air, turns the sky to stone. No ground either for the house or for any of those pedestrians waiting there. To be sure, their firmly planted feet suggest a plane, but a plane for each one of them – therefore no possible place or an infinity of planes in a delirium of space. Everything in this astonishing picture is fixed except the structure of space. Mystery? Magritte uttered the word. He challenged mystery, defied it, played with it. He did not wait religiously for mystery to seep down to him and invade him. He held out his hand to it. He dominated it by a kind of feline intellectuality. We understand so well the usual order of things: to perceive is to depend upon

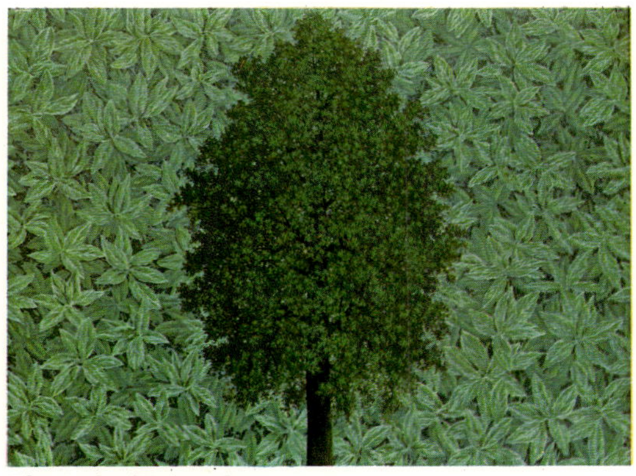

The Arch of Triumph
Gouache 1962 / 10.6 × 13.8

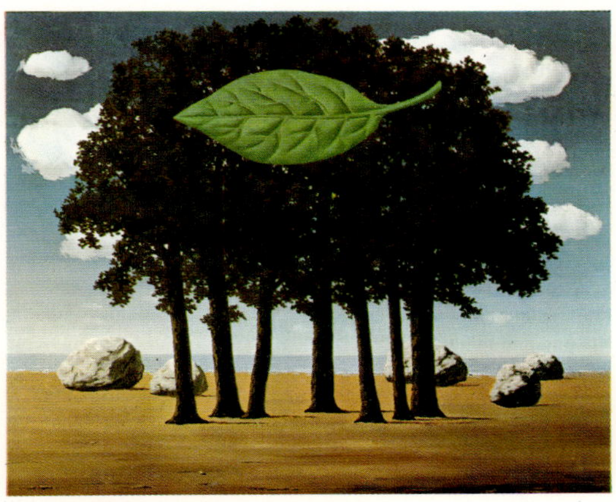

The Tablets of the Law
About 1950 / 25.6 × 31.5

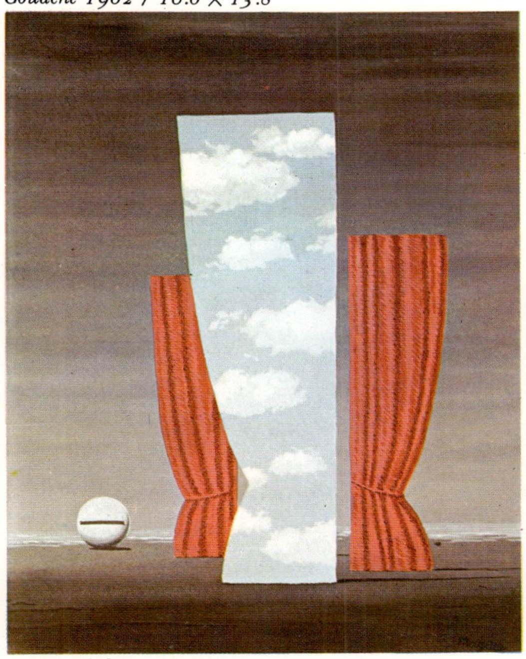

La Giaconda
Gouache 1964 / 10.6 × 13.8

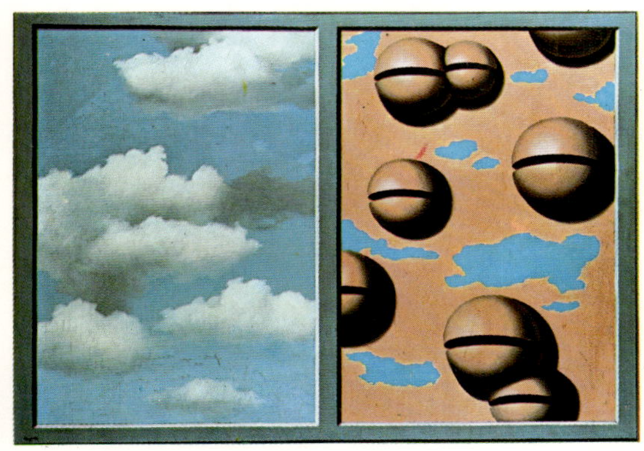

Pink Bells, Tattered Skies
1930 / 28.8 × 39.4

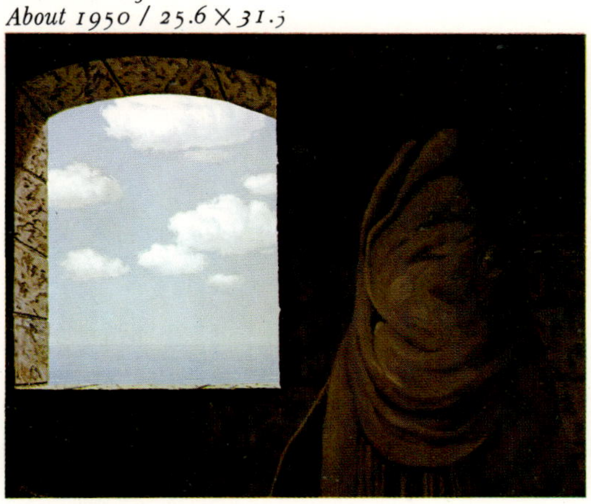

Gloria
1966 / 25.6 × 31.5

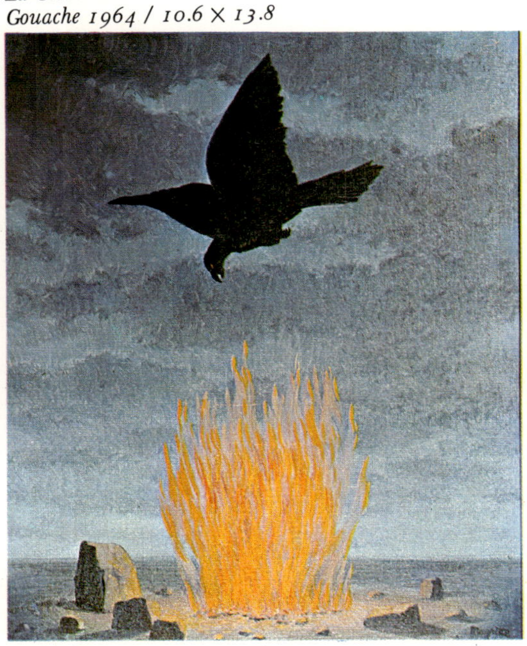

The Fanatics
1955 / 23.6 × 19.8

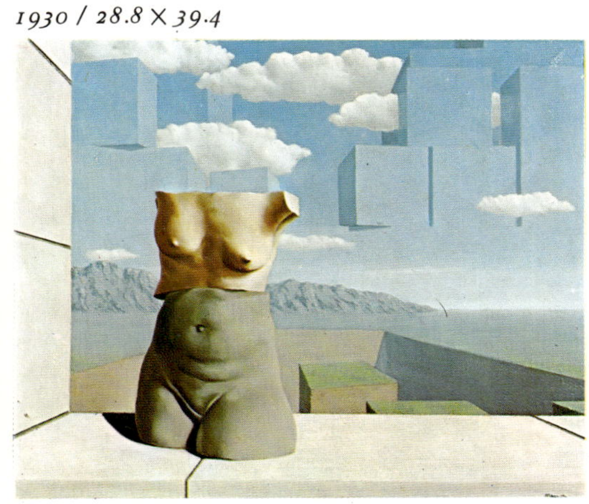

The March of Summer
1938 / 23.6 × 28.8

the logic of the world. Magritte attacked, intellectually, that comfortable perception. His "systematic disarrangement of all the senses" had nothing to do with the image – he had only to take drugs, absinthe or mescaline. No, he attacked the inner order and the logic of the perceived. How, with that idiotic self-sufficiency, can we trust the logic of our senses? Transgressed, doubted, it appears more clearly in all its mystery.

From the glowing Chirico and his enigmas to the mystery that haunts Magritte, the painter-poets of objects in space are not complaisant towards the world. Under pretext of questioning it, they almost insolently force it to suffer a sort of revealing outrage. If that questioning is fundamental, do not expect them to give us an explanation. It comes from the depths where the sources of anguish are hidden. Is there no mystery in man too? The mystery of the logic of the world sends us back to the mystery of the mind as the painter daily experiences its obscurity in his tenacious efforts to develop his work. Then what of the space within? To Magritte it is a nocturnal space.

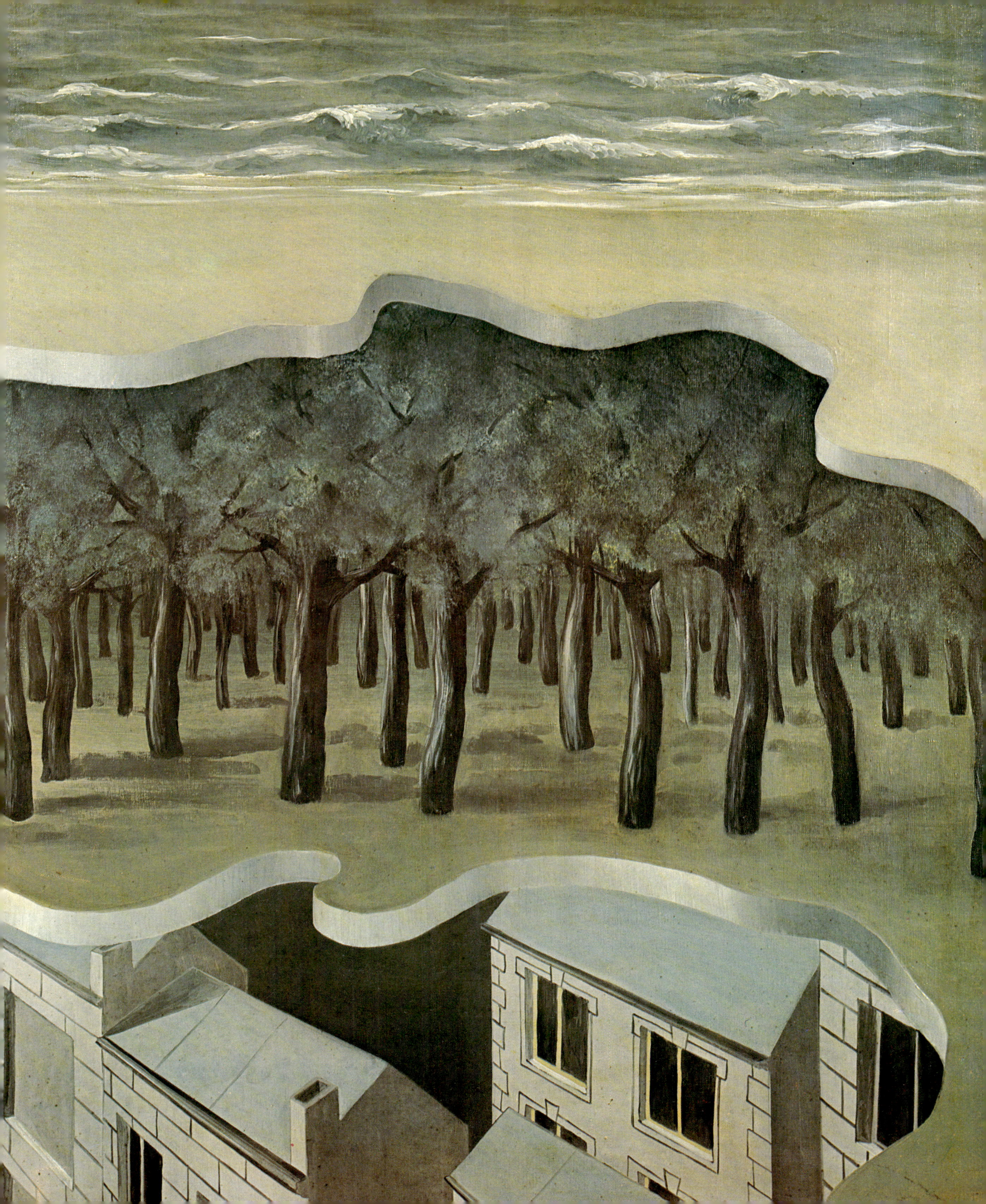

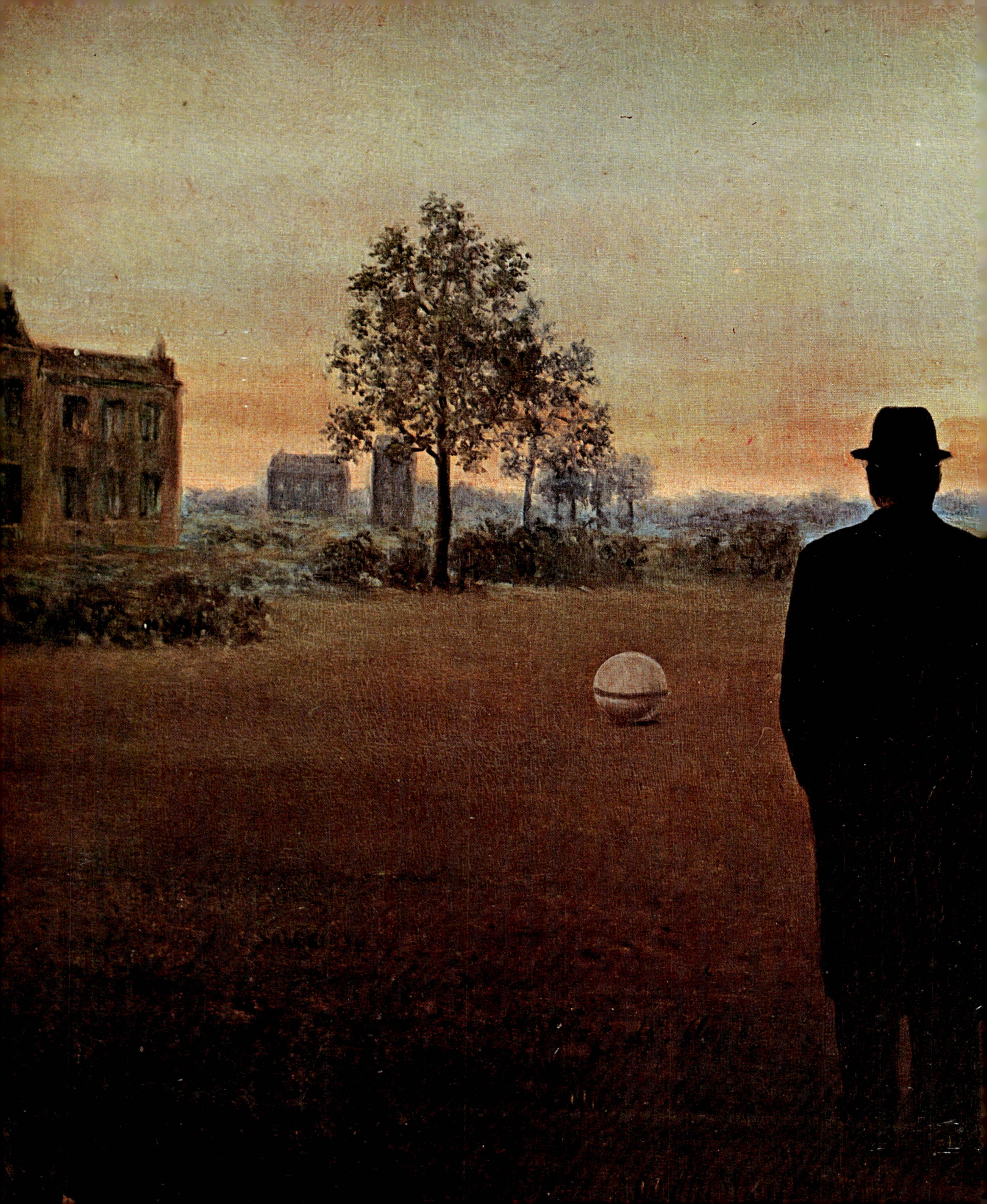

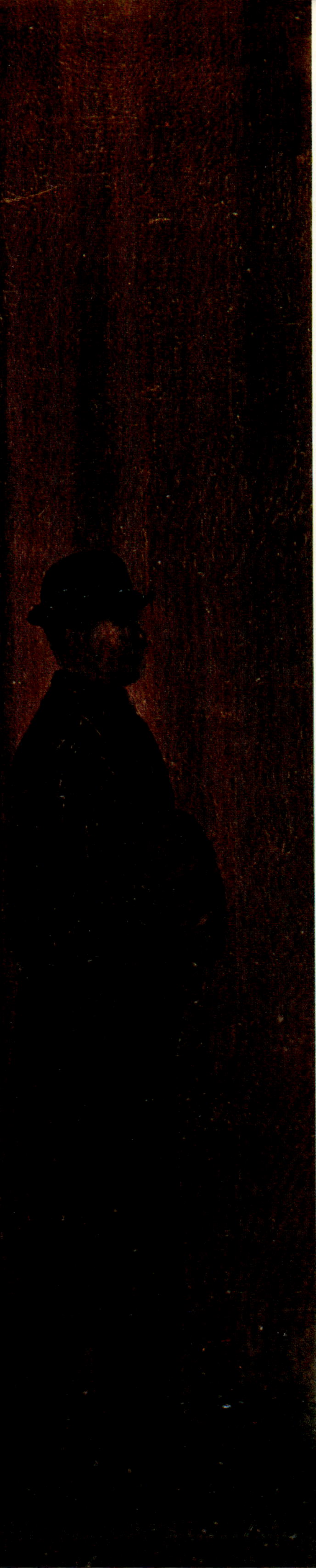

Gaspard de la Nuit
1965 / 25.6 × 31.5

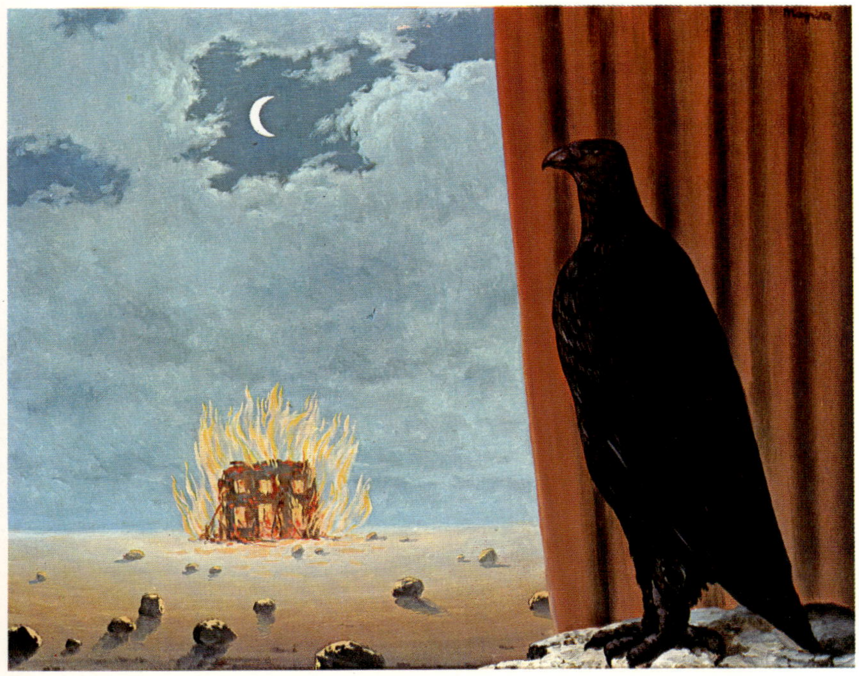

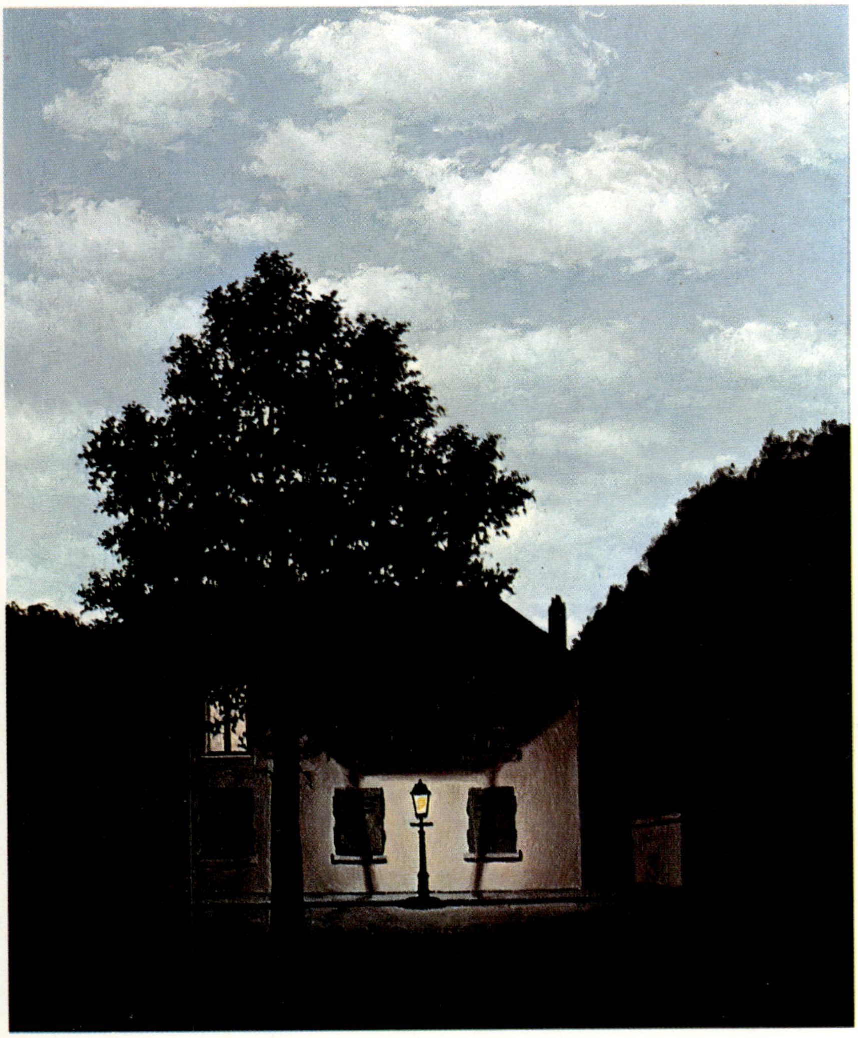

Empire of Light
About 1958 / 39.4 × 31.5

Opposite page:
Going Towards Pleasure
1950 / 19.3 × 22.8

White Night
1928 or 1929 / 21.2 × 28.8

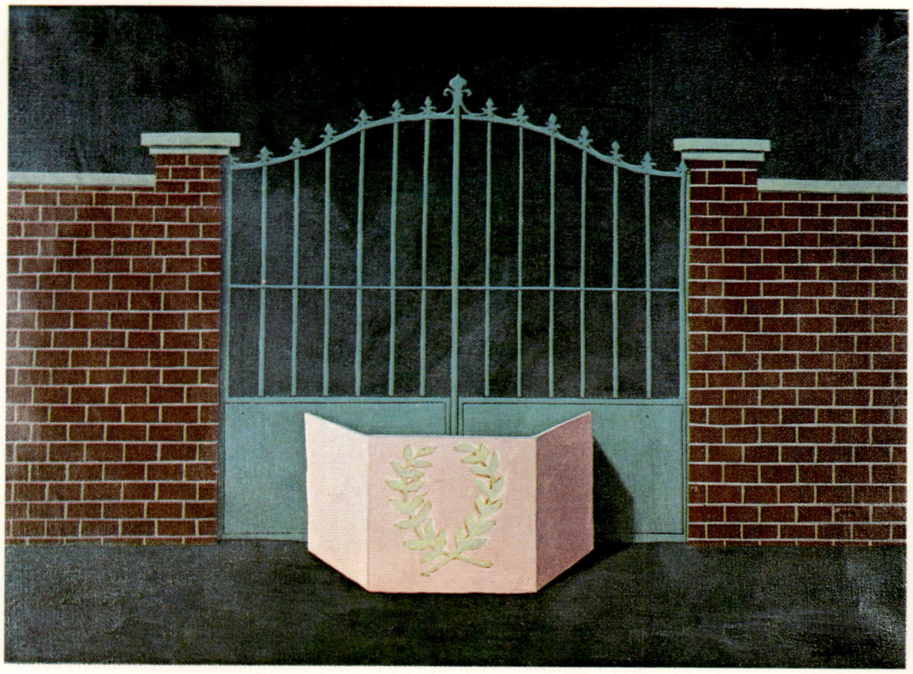

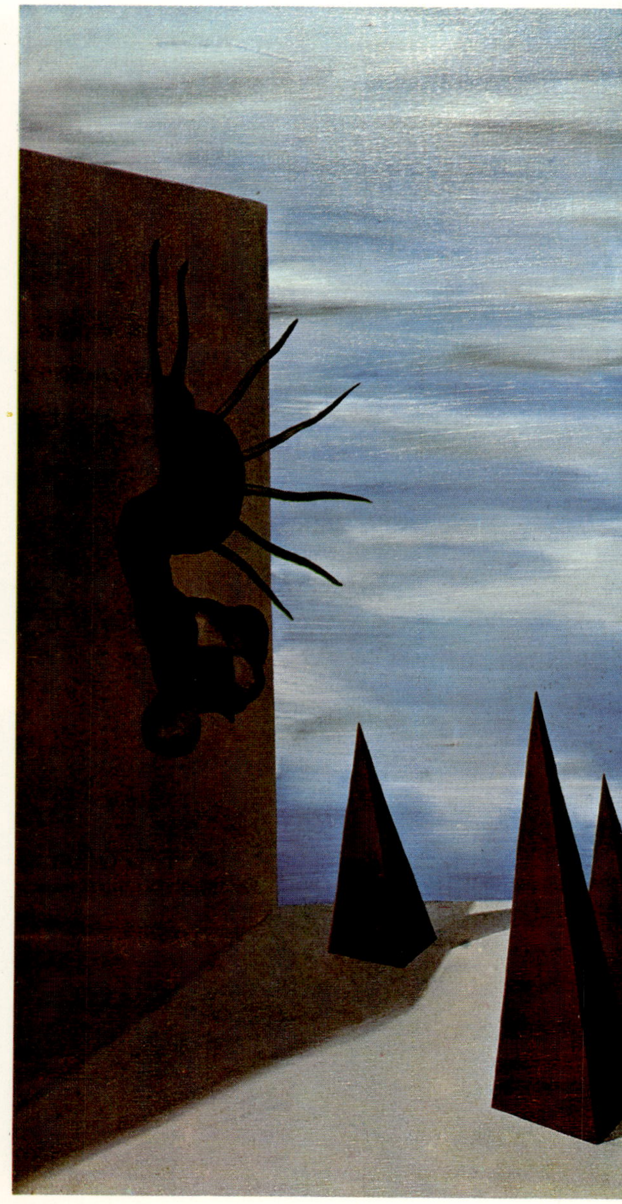

The Monster's Walk (detail)
1926-1927 / 32.3 × 15.8

Opposite page:
The Musings of a Solitary Walker
1926-1927 / 54.3 × 42.5

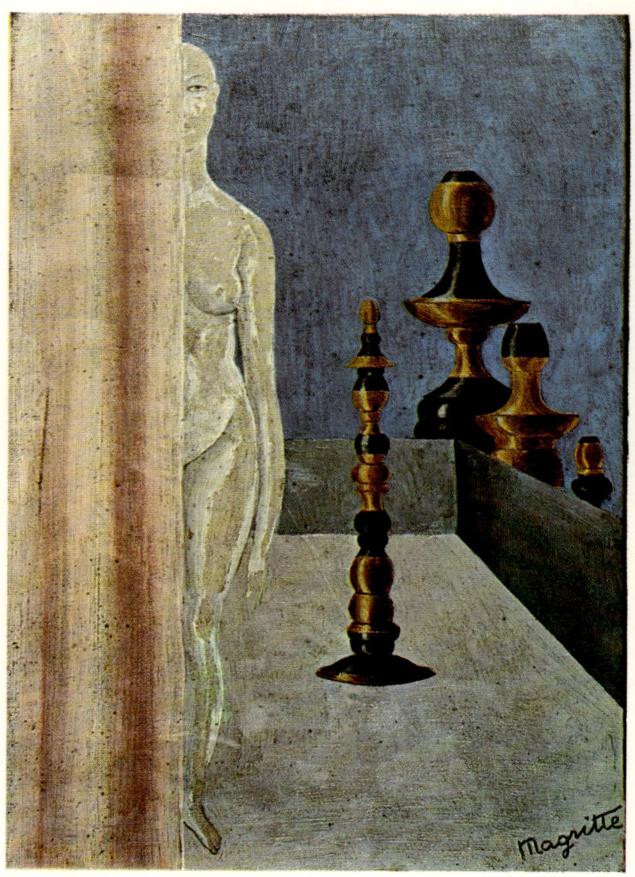

The Terrace at Ata Hiralpa
1925 / 19.8 × 13.8

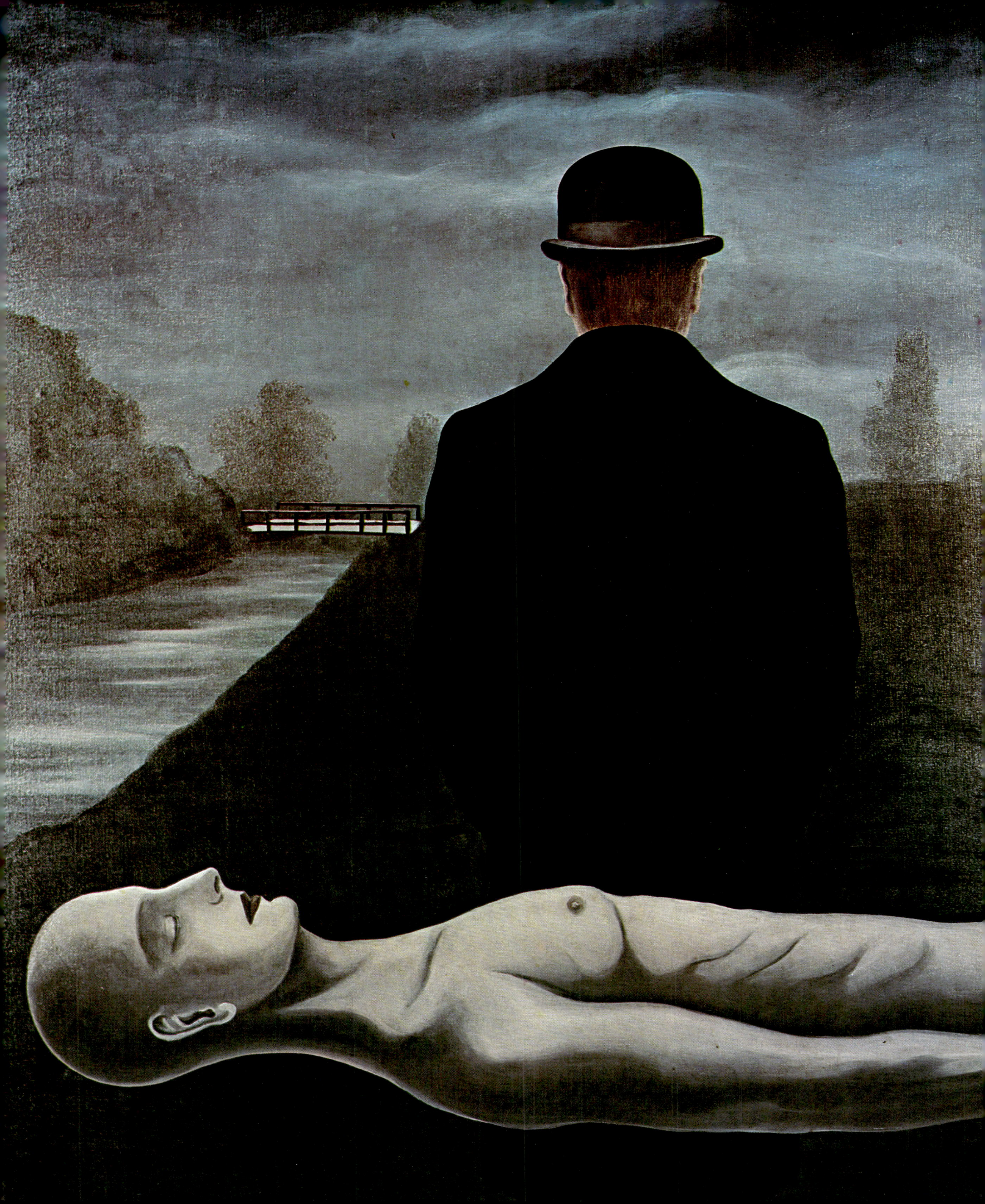

2 THE INNER NIGHT

Surrealism
will introduce you to mortality,
which is a secret society.
It will glove your hand
burying in it
the deep M
with which the word
Memory begins.

André Breton, "First Manifesto," *(les Manifestes du surréalisme)*, Paris, Ed. du Sagittaire, 1946, p. 55.

Magritte is not a neurotic. All evidence of his cold ecstasy to the contrary, his paintings would not be considered masterpieces because of their unconscious and symbolic admission of latent conflicts or of impulses derived obscurely from the libido. Besides, the general problem of psychoanalyzing art or artists through their works is far from being positively resolved. We know that though the surrealists have claimed kinship with psychoanalysis, Freud "did not understand anything about surrealists." The painter expresses himself, no doubt, but his self-analysis appears impossible to the most scientifically serious men who maintain psychiatric technique at the level of a dialogue between the doctor and his patient. All art is a delusion and the artist never admits it. We are therefore scarcely disposed to claim that a specialized reading of Magritte's works would reveal indications of symbols unknown to the painter himself and significant of what he was hiding from himself.

However, Magritte's attitude towards psychoanalysis, that almost horrified refusal which undoubtedly did not exclude a certain fear, tempts one to indiscretion.

"Art as I conceive of it," he wrote, "does not take kindly to psychoanalysis. It evokes the mystery without which the world would not exist, that is to say, the mystery that must not be confused with a problem, as difficult as that may be" (1). In contrast to Salvador Dali, who claimed that he was helped in his plastic creations by sleep, Magritte fled divination through dreams. "I am careful to paint only pictures that evoke the mystery of the world. To do that I must be wide awake." Magritte never pursued automatism or spontaneity, which is the major prescription of surrealism and his proclamation of "full sunlight" undoubtedly had much to do with his estrangement from the author of *Vases communicants*. Contrary to Duchamp and to several other chess players, Magritte's inventiveness follows the path of a slow calculation, traversed by lighting flashes.

Full sunlight? In his "Renoir period" without any doubt. But the ensemble of his work, with elements of dull color scales, was to remain dedicated to cold colors. In that *Leçons de choses* style the light effects are unaffected by light. Except when it is night. The different versions of *l'Empire des lumières* are all nocturnal. A gas-lamp lights the façade and the clarity of the sky re-enforces the darkness of the foliage... Magritte's secret night is that of a forest interior in the moonlight. Crack the surface of a woman's body and houses appear inside. Magritte even painted a three-storied picture, open like the model of a house, three levels to which the psychologist promptly gives names in his language. Above, the sea laps quietly on the shore: this is the strata of serenity and the infinite. Below appears the interior of the forest where Magritte so often lingers. There the trees are solidly planted in the semi-darkness. At the bottom of the picture, the mystery of a life appears: empty houses. No curtains at the windows, no smoke issuing from the chimneys, nobody. How then can we help recalling that strange childhood, the many moves from one place to another (Lessines, Gilly, Châtelet, Charleroi) and the tragedy of a night when the whole household searched for the mother who had disappeared, who had thrown herself into the Sambre? The child of fourteen protected himself against his wound by false pride at being, in the eyes of his pals, "the son of the woman who committed suicide." False coldness! Against that loss of his mother, Magritte was to erect the harrier of his unique love for Georgette Berger, whom he met one year after the tragedy, then lost, found again and married. The empty house is one of Magritte's sinister themes. In his canvas *la Poitrine*, he was to go so far as to crowd together in an absurdness that points to despair the whole pile of hollow buildings. The more constant theme of the double is less marked by sadness than by derision. Who is that character in a bowler, often seen from the back, sometimes a phantom-like silhouette dwelling in branches? When by chance, he turns towards us, an apple hides his face. Ridiculous! He is always motionless, dreaming, dressed to the nines. There he is, everywhere in the sky, glued to the open window. He is often quite alone or duplicated. In *A la Rencontre du Plaisir*, one man in profile emerges from the picture, disappears in the shadow; the other, with his back to us, is looking at a vague piece of ground in which that always horizontally cleft sphere is set exactly in the middle, a kind of silent bell, matrix, and money-box, spatial device and maternal symbol which Magritte repeats in all his works. If this little shopkeeper is the painter's double does not Magritte root him out in his desire not to be a sedentary suburbanite, lover of operettas and Pomeranians, but an artist? "The Magrittes," writes Patrick Waldberg," have always fled from Bohemian types. In their most difficult periods they would not allow themselves to show either their embarrassment or their artistic calling." (2). Artist! A surrealist cannot let himself be taken in by the "ridiculous idea of an artistic career." Even less the surrealist painter, the most inclined, by his irony and his caustic tongue, to share the jeers of Dada at the seriousness of art... Behind that well-dressed gentleman lies the body of the true "I" who wanted to be an artist even though art is dead. In the distance a wooden bridge spans the canal. Is it meant to pass from one bank to the other, from this too well-dressed living man to that cold dead man and vice versa? Or (like another man) so that he can lean over the handrail and throw himself in the water? If the man in the bowler went down there to make proper use of that bridge (the bridge between men, which is art as everyone knows) he would experience that majestic death, he bears in his shadow. *Promeneur solitaire*, dead to the world, dead to himself, dead to social vanities, dead to art. Is not the theme of death the one Magritte treats most constantly, the continuous base of his inner music? We find it in every chapter of this book. "Death, let us not speak of that," he said. But memory, repudiated in that head of marble, lets a drop of blood seep through "and the temple is wet with the memory of an old tragedy." (3). In truth, death is less the end of a life that returns to melt into the "mystery of the world" – there are few decomposed forms in Magritte's works – than the permanent law of a vision which constantly reduces the living being to the thing, the thing to its fragment, in icy petrification. Magritte's make-believe plays on a descending

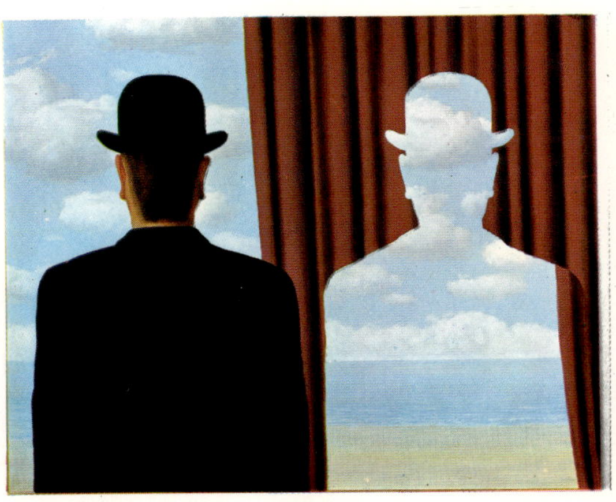

Transfer
1966 / 31.9 × 39.4

vertical line. Derision is accompanied by bewilderment. Breton has condemned one of Tzara's paintings – *guitar, a singing bidet* – as being degrading and debasing. "The surrealist picture," he writes, "should be characterized by the analogy of an ascending symbol." (4). Magritte is certainly nearer to Tzara than to Breton and, with the machinery of Picabia, he recovers that sense of combinative mechanics that Duchamp carried so far. In *l'Age des Merveilles*, the woman in the shroud who faces us, displays the mechanism of a watch in her stomach. If one day a spring broke in René Magritte's inner night – and everything then congealed in a void – he would

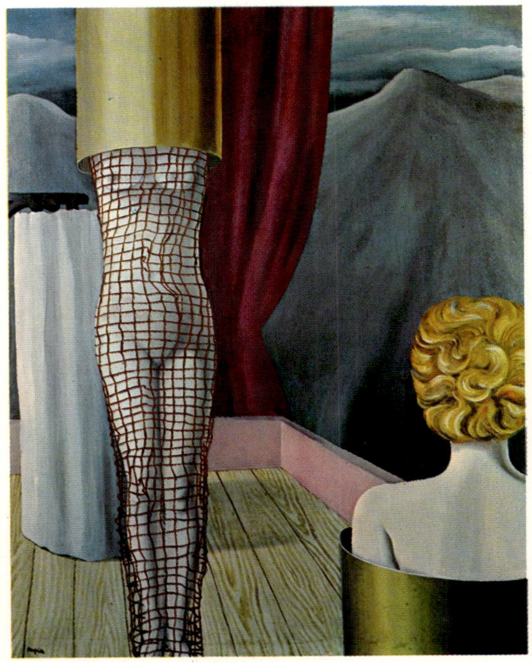

The Magician's Accomplices
1927 / 41.3 × 15.8

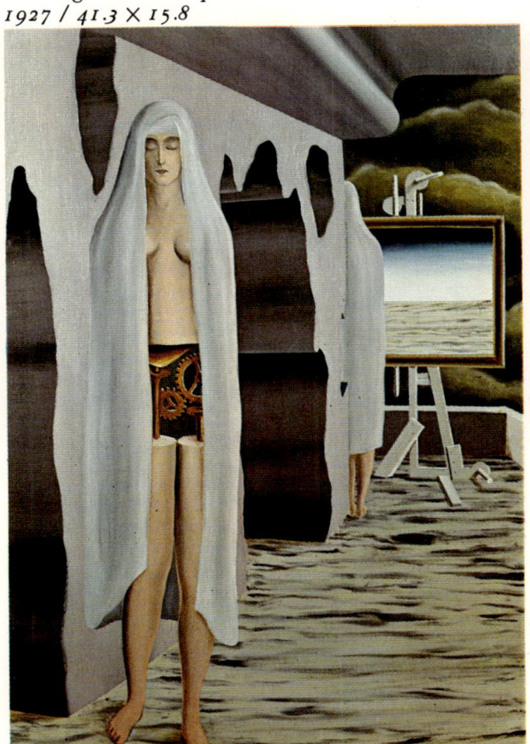

The Age of Marvels
1926 / 45.6 × 31.9

protect himself from any inner destruction that might have resulted by casting a similar break on the world. What Scutenaire considers "a son of boredom" is not worn away by the spleen of Vaché, the "what's-the-use" that undermines all power. Magritte is still the high-strung child who frightened his father's servants by excessive mimicries of his adolescent piety, he is still the impetuous youth who began to paint as much as a canvas a day once he had found, in 1925, the path that the *Jockey perdu* opened up to him. His coldness is secondary. Through it the artist in him dominates the man and saves him. It reduces the world to the level of the most intimate misfortune, the one that leaves you without tears, unable to weep, and to which you can only say: "It is too absurd." In his painting, Magritte

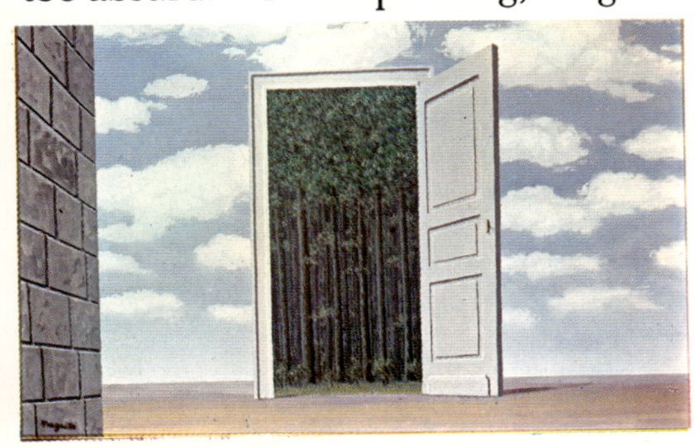

The Child Found Again
1966 / 11.8 × 15.8

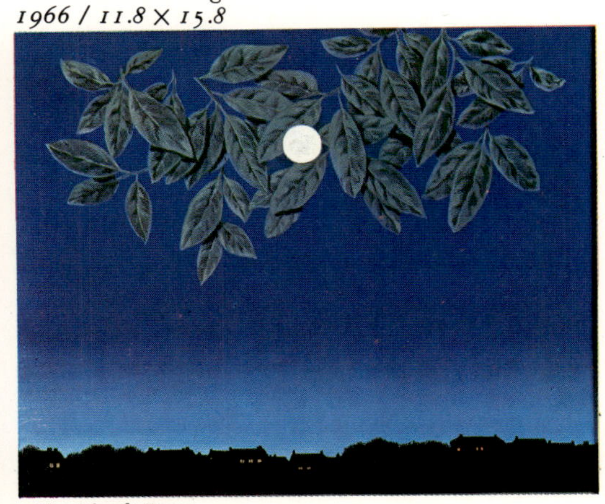

The Blank Page
1967 / 21.2 × 25.6

dissects, with surgical patience, the absurdity of the world. Now, in the center of that world, there is a woman.

(1) Brussels, May 21, 1962, in "The Vision of René Magritte," catalogue of the exhibition at Walker Art Center, Minneapolis, Sept.-Oct., 1962.
(2) "René Magritte," Brussels, André de Rache, 1965, p. 188.
(3) Henri Michaux: *En rêvant à partir de peintures énigmatiques*, Mercure de France, Dec. 1964, p. 186.
(4) A. Breton, Signe ascendant, "Neon," No I. 1947. Reprinted as preface in the collection *Signe ascendant*, Paris, Gallimard, 1968, coll. Poésie.

The Schoolteacher
1954 / 31.5 × 25.6

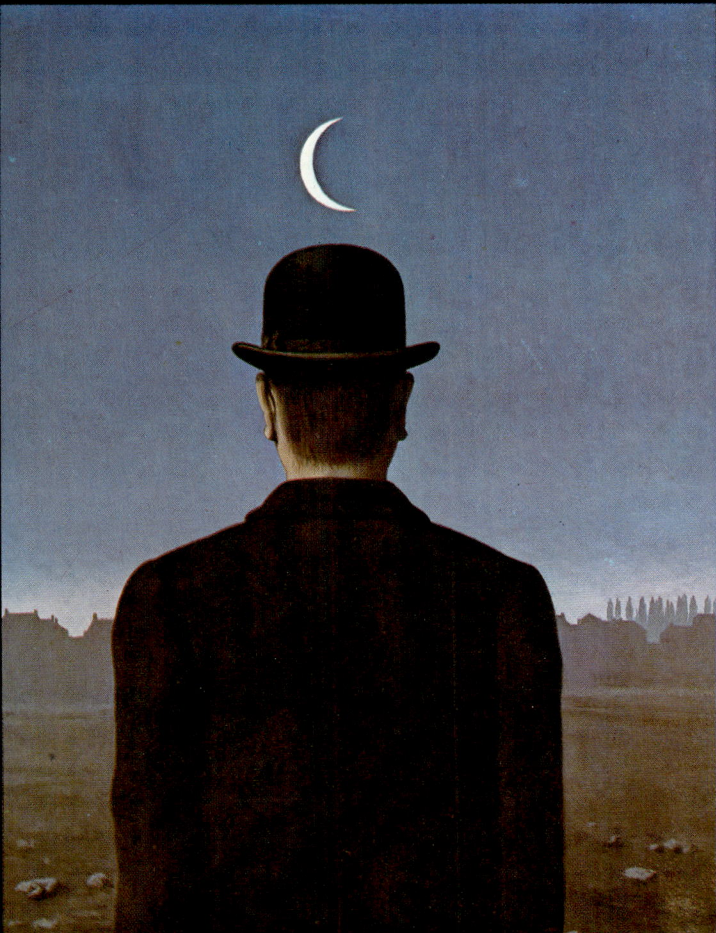

The Evening Gown
1954 / 31.5 × 23.6

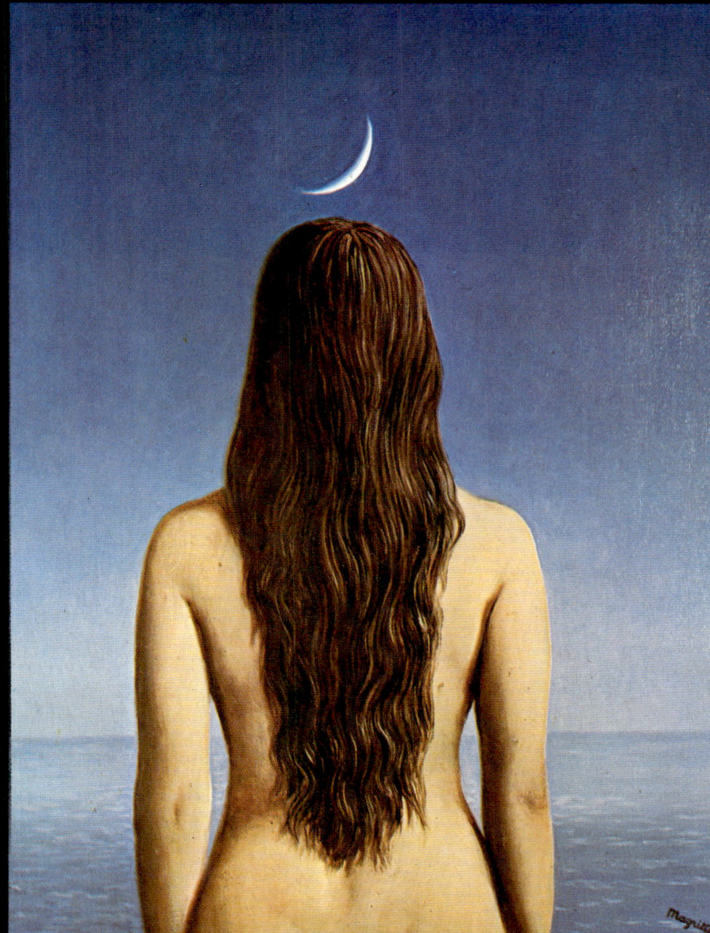

3. WOMAN OBSERVED

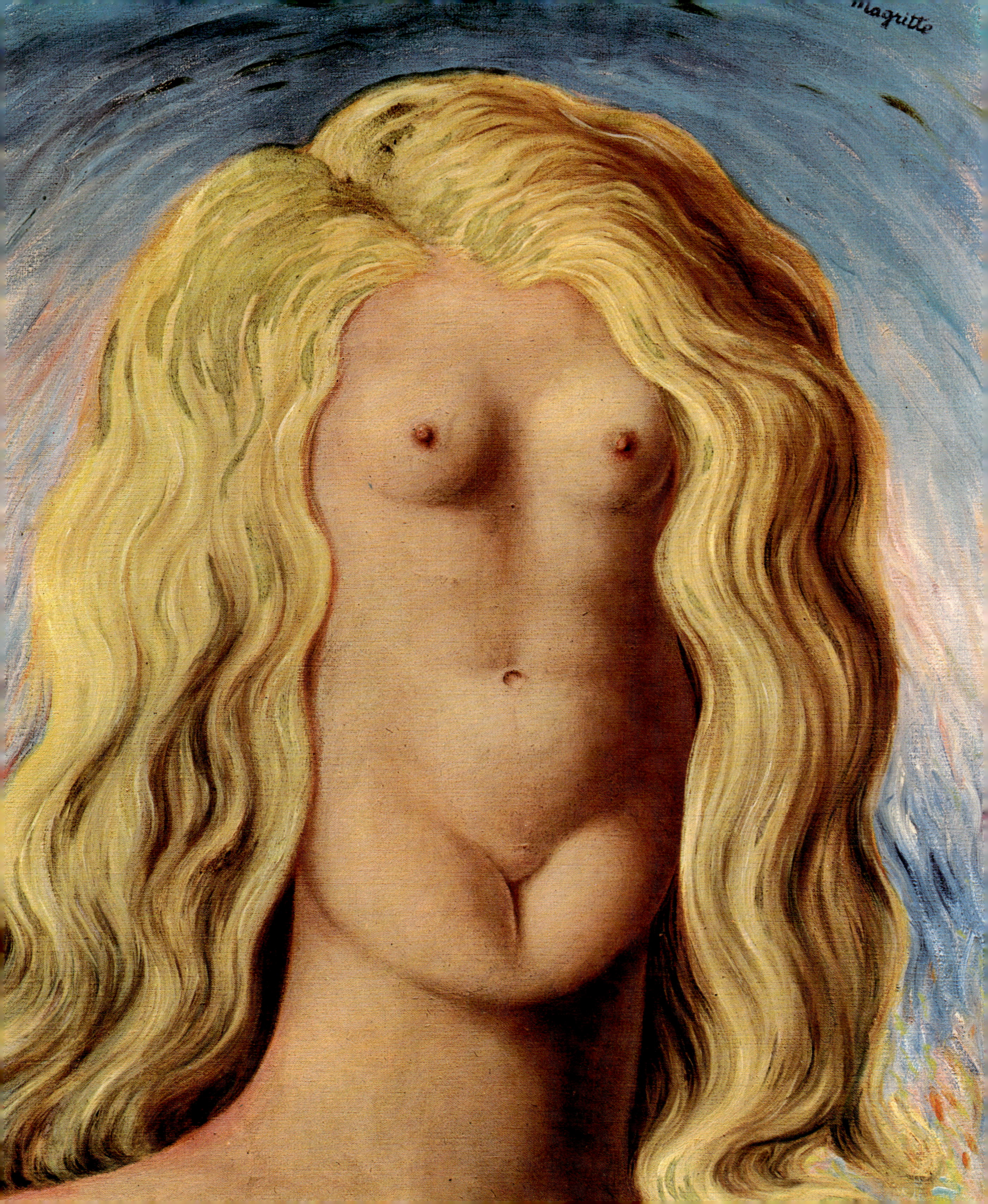
Magritte

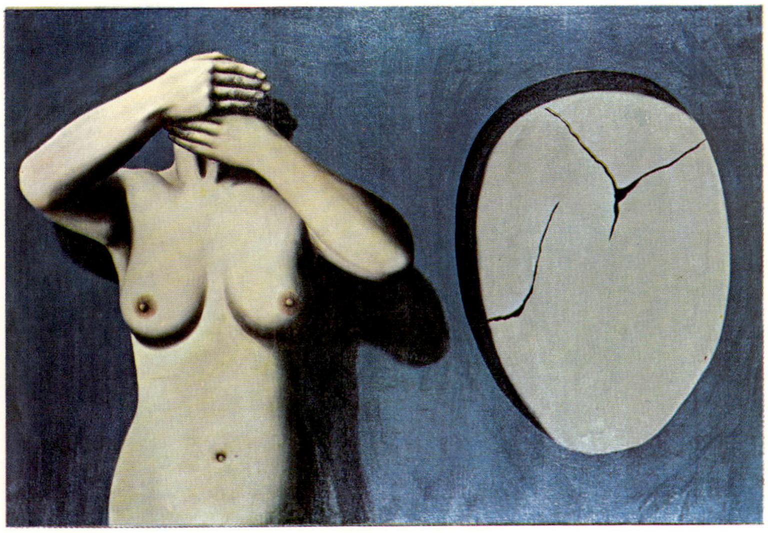

The Nocturnal Kind
1928 / 31.5 × 45.1

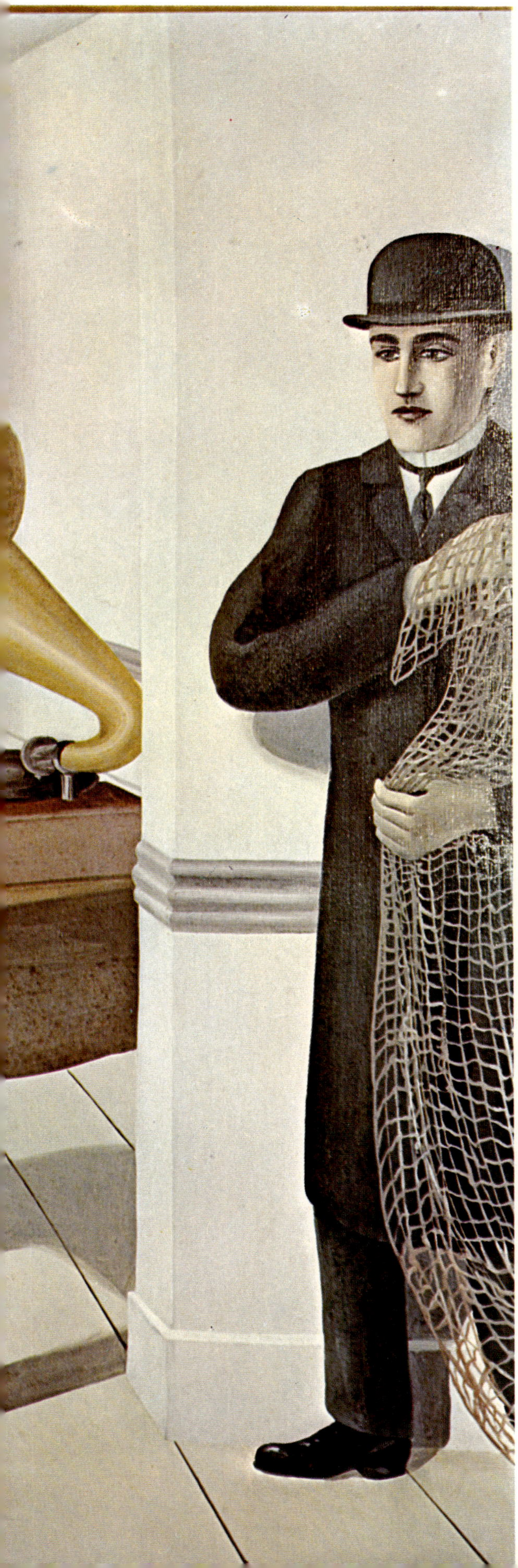

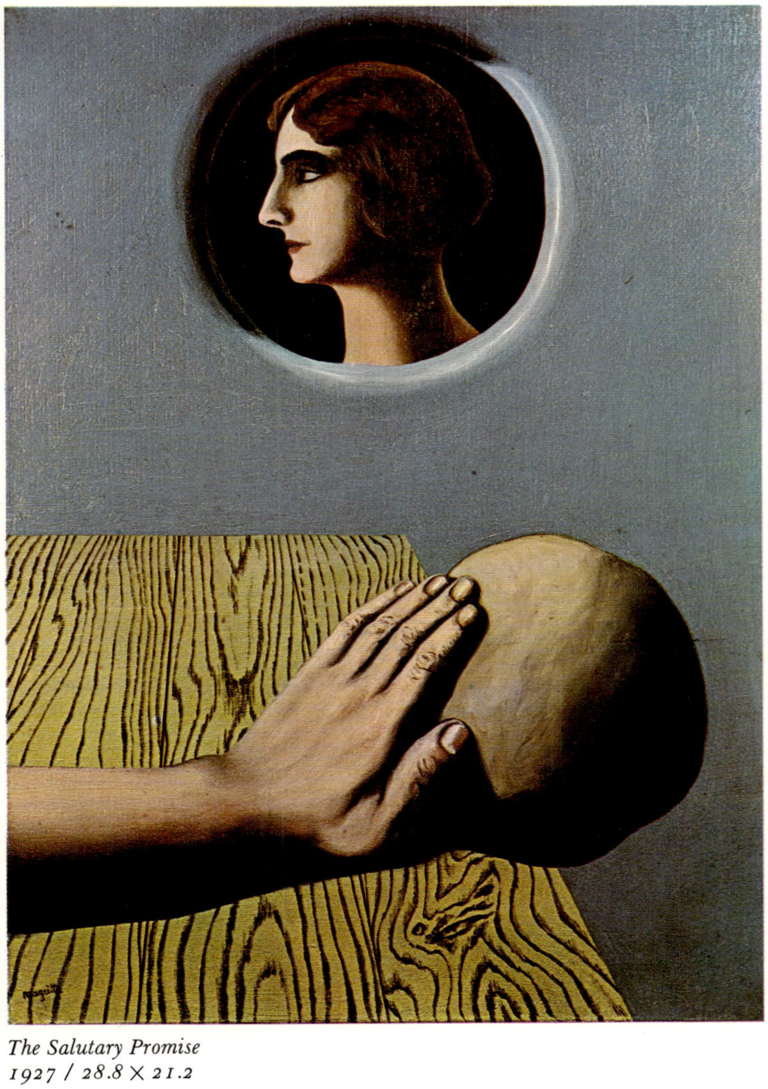

The Salutary Promise
1927 / 28.8 × 21.2

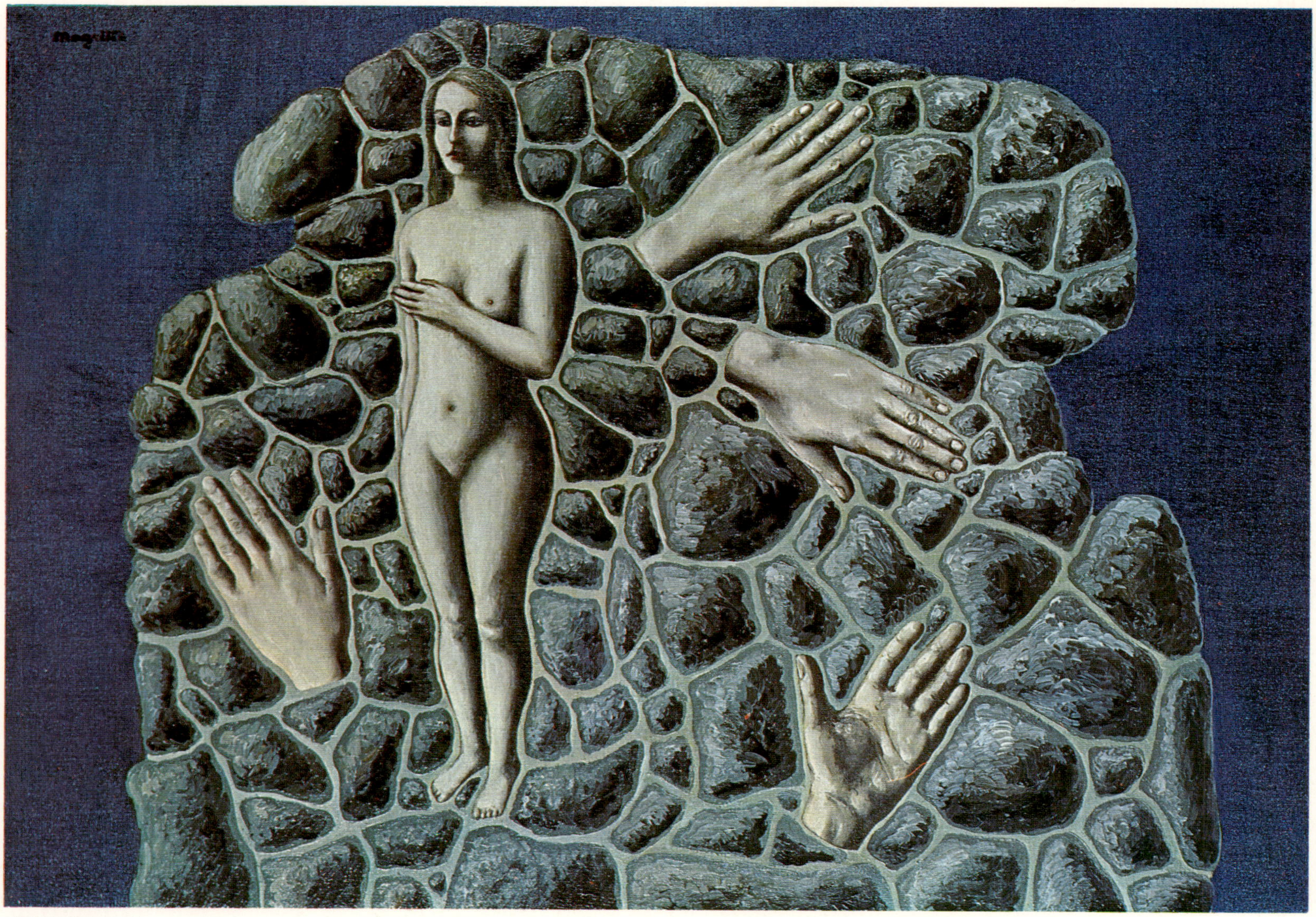

Find the Woman!
1927 / 31.9 × 45.6

Opposite page:
Ready-made Bouquet
1956 / 25.6 × 19.6

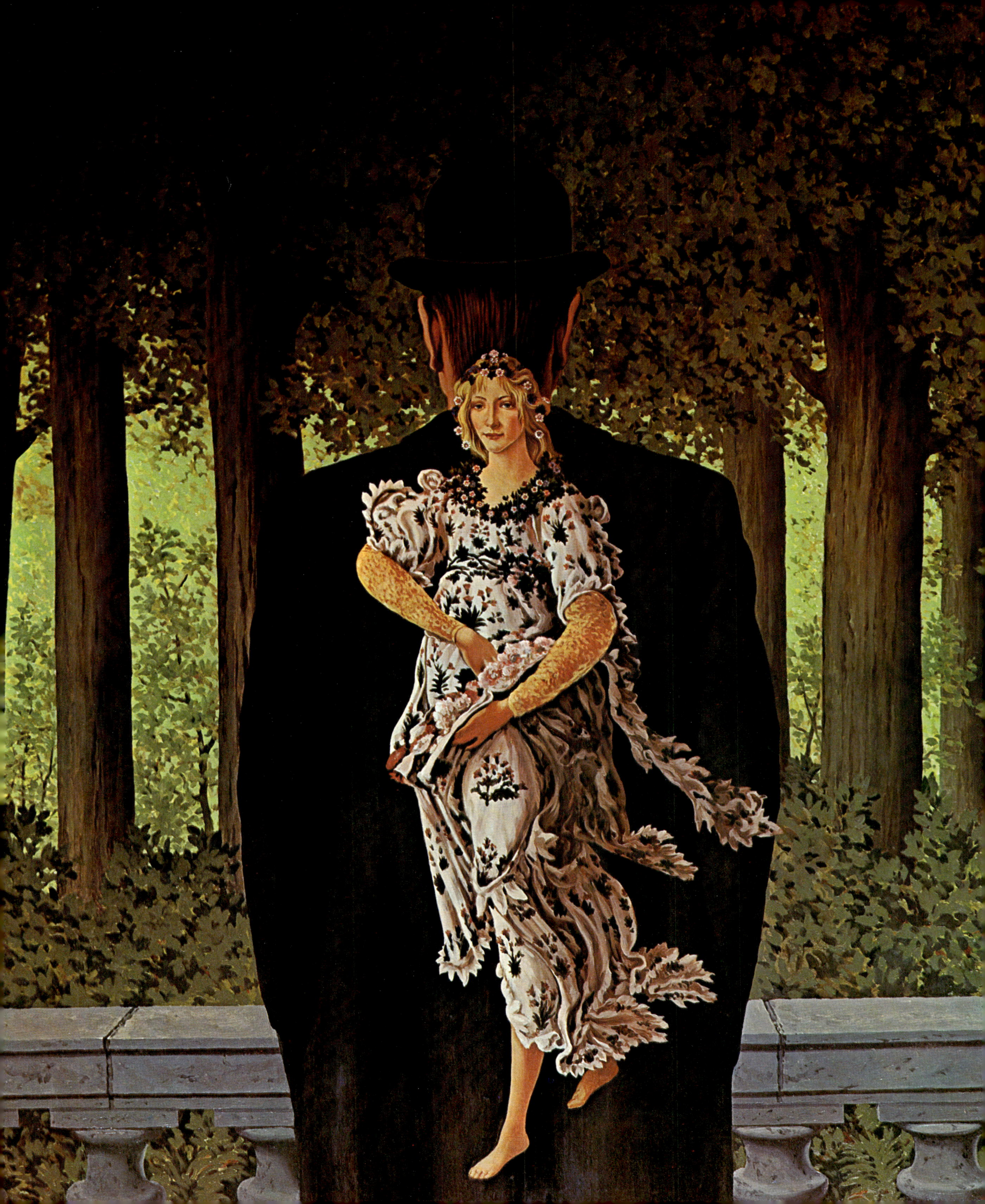

3 WOMAN OBSERVED

I persist in mingling fictions
with formidable realities.
Houses unlived in,
I have peopled you with
exceptional women
neither fat, nor thin, blonde nor dark,
mad nor wise, it matters little,
but with women more alluring than
could be, by a detail.
Useless objects,
Even the folly that led to your
fabrication
was a source of delights to me.

Paul Eluard, *la Vie immédiate,* Paris, les Chaiers libres, 1932.

Naked. Rarely does some anecdotal figure wear a robe. Nudity is an ontological attribute of woman (as for the Aphrodite of the Greeks), whereas the male is clad from head to toe in the armor of his respectability. Magritte's naked woman is in general like marble. Not very lascivious, even chaste. She seems to pose in her cold beauty, with exquisite gestures. A studio piece for the painter's eye. Woman observed. The couple holds less mystery for Magritte (there are few couples in his paintings) than this woman, kept at a distance propitious to the eye's sensual desire. A prey of the *voyeur?* No, she is materialized, immobile, whereas the *voyeur,* the Peeping Tom, is on the lookout for nothing so much as the movements (and the most intimate movements possible) of the woman who thinks she is unobserved... Let us follow Magritte's eyes.

First of all, here are the clothes: a dress on a coat-hanger and shoes she has taken off, the very opposite of a naked woman. But through a fetishistic hallucination, breasts and toes appear on that linen which comes to life instead of following Magritte's bent towards petrification. A less exceptional picture than one might think in the context of a revery on the woman-object—purposely so-called with reference to Sade (1)—its connection with the naked woman reminds us that the absent one, whose clothes we are looking at, is always undressed: indeed, even in her finery, nudity is woman's essential element. The nudity of her body, hieratic object, in other words, holy, inviolate. Whence rape. To meditate on the human face is an exercise dear to all those who make a supreme value of the person; and the man who falls in love with a woman's personal appearance knows her first through an exchange of glances and sighs. The way to love is through the face: its fulfillment through the body. That is why "admirable love" is addressed to the whole woman, face and body, all in one block but never intermingled, all of her. On the contrary far from being a sublimation of the body, that slipping of the torso on the face (the breasts look at you, the nose atrophies and becomes a navel, the mouth-pubis appears drawn into a painful grimace) is a desecration of the face which has become a sexual object, blind, deaf and mute. It follows the movement of transgression downward which is one of Magritte's constant themes. But here are more disturbing forms. With Magritte, the sadistic themes, which most surrealist painters have made the essential core of their homage to woman, exclude the carnal entanglements of Bellmer as well as the bleedings of Labisse. The spot of blood that stains the temple of a marble statue is a wound of memory, not a revery of desire. Magritte's pictorial sadism is the sadism of blows received by an inert victim. Most often those imaginary blows leave no trace, nor does the fire burn up the trombone or the chair. The total petrification of the woman observed satisfies Magritte's oneiric cruelty. When he cuts a woman in half, she is of plaster or cardboard. In *la Folie des grandeurs* (1961) he makes a kind of Russian doll out of an ancient torso, whose three hollow pieces fit one into the other... Reification that borders on the ridiculous! Here he is making fun of painting (the idea of the picture) as well as the woman in this nude cut up into five pictures superimposed one upon the other. After all one could hang them on the wall in a more fanciful order. Magritte agrees with Sartre in the way he looks at woman: a look that "pursues the death of the other one." He kills the person to magnify the object. He even goes so far as to transfix the object, to strike it, to cut it up, to pass on his vertical derision, his aggressive sense of the absurd through the most beautiful creature in the world, the mediatrix, the fairy, the source of the marvelous. But, such are the contradictions of man, Magritte loves woman. The cold attention he brings to bear on her, places her at the heart of the mystery of "what is." She is enigmatic, she is beautiful. Her body and her face equally serene, are often motionless. A dove on her shoulder, a subtle flexing of a hip, a slight gesture, make woman a sorceress. Silent as to her secret, we are concerned only with her. In her presence we have good grounds for feeling guilty. Magritte's man, with his bowler and his clothes that make him so stiff, is a man punished. He often turns his back on us as though he were standing in a corner, forbidden to move.

And this is the strange nightmare of *l'Assassin menacé* (1926). A naked woman is laid out on a couch. She has been murdered (a thin stream of blood trickles from her mouth). Murdered by whom? By the man who seems to be listening to a verdict on the gramaphone? He is listening to his master's voice – or to his mistress's. In the background three witnesses, bareheaded like the murderer, are leaning on the sill and looking through the window. In the foreground, on each side, stand two men in mufti, each wearing a bowler, one of them armed with a club, the other with a net. All the men have their eyes open and all of them face us. Only the prostrate and very desirable victim has her eyes closed. A piece of clothing is pulled up to her neck: she must have been raped. Who is threatening the lover-murderer? The two armed men? The voice of his conscience? Is it not rather the naked woman by her very nakedness, inert, eternal, beyond reach, omnipotent? The nightmare is infallible. Those petty bourgeois raised to the rank of judges are ludicrous, but the man who murdered the naked woman is going to die. For through her immobile nakedness, the woman observed is a human being, the very soul of the inaccessible. The eye seeks to kill her and almost reaches her; the hand, sensual or brutal, never touches her. Her body is sacred, inviolable. In the canvas so well entitled *la Femme introuvable,*

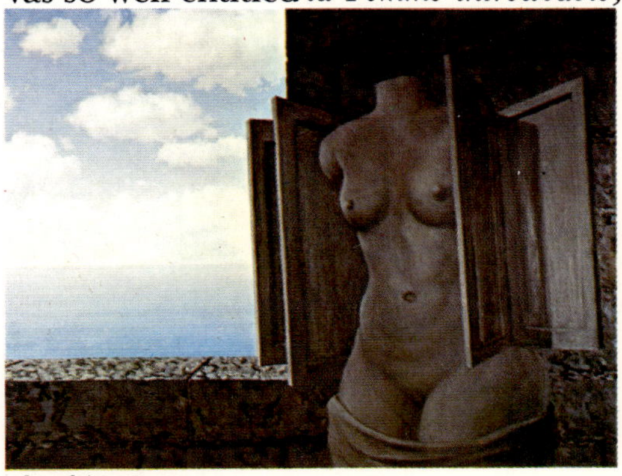

The Flying Statue
1963 / 31.5 × 39.4

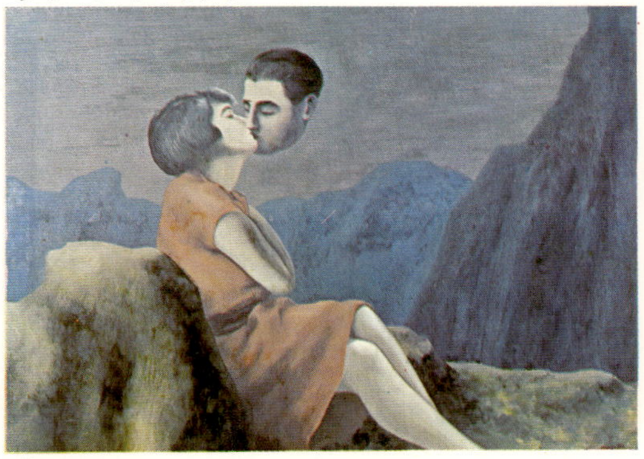

The Lovers
1928 / 21.2 × 28.8

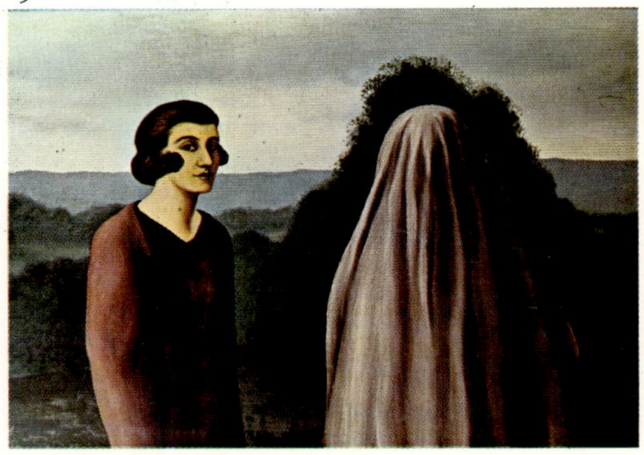

The Invention of Life
1926 / 31.5 × 47.5

hands never cease to search for those other hands that nevertheless remain serenely at rest, but visible. And one thinks of Magritte's montage: "I do not see the naked woman hidden in the forest (2) in which all the surrealists, photographed with their eyes closed, surround a naked woman who is, however, well worth seeing if any one

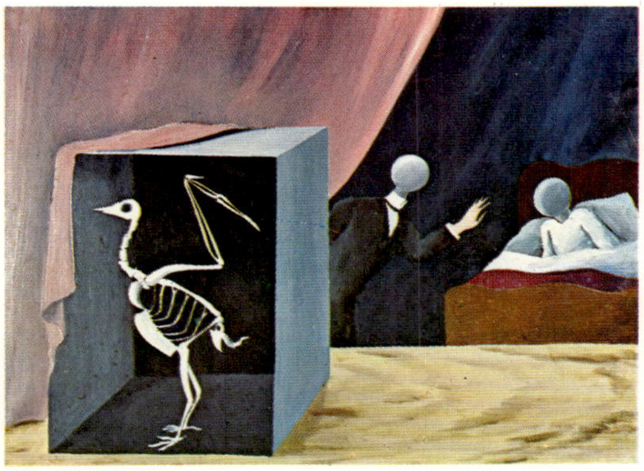

The Big News
1926 / 24.4 × 31.5

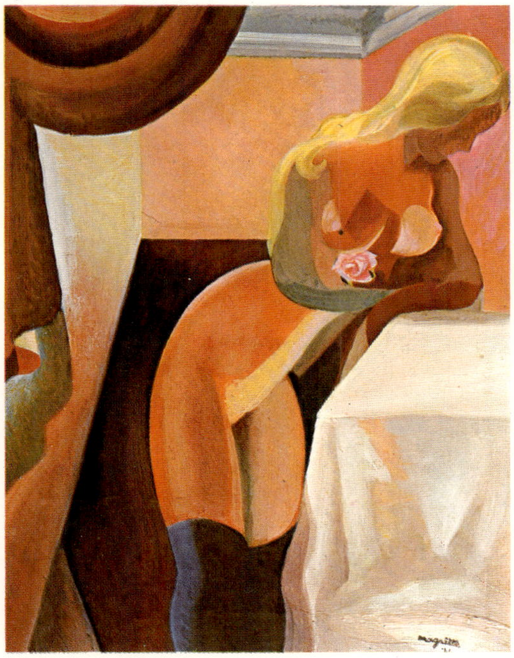

Woman with the Rose
1924 / 21.6 × 15.8

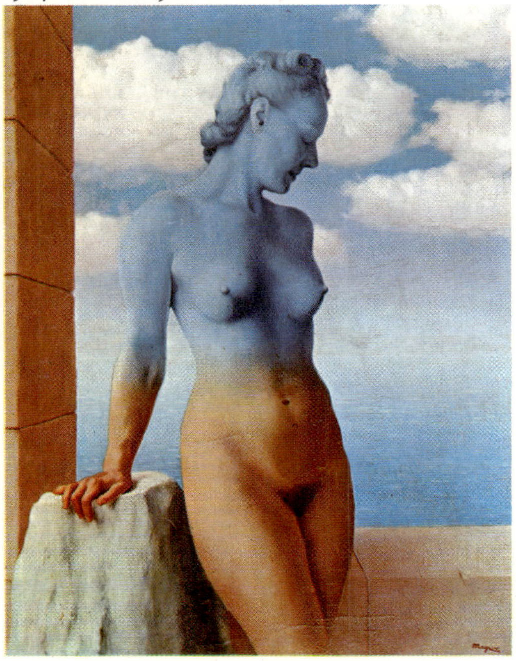

Black Magic
1935 / 31.5 × 23.6

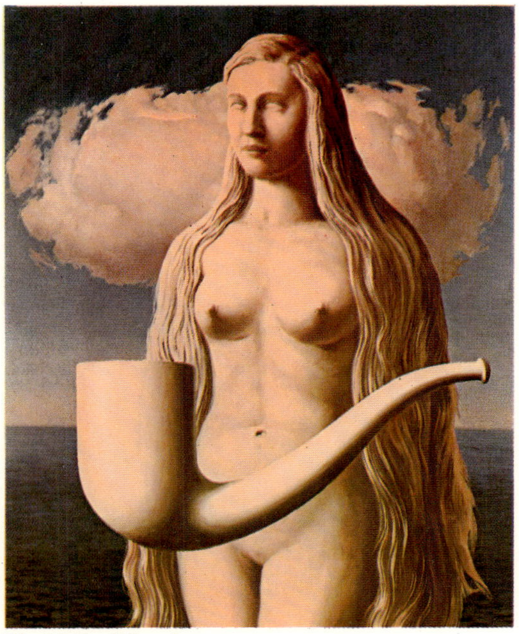

The Mask of Thunder
1967 / 31.5 × 25.6

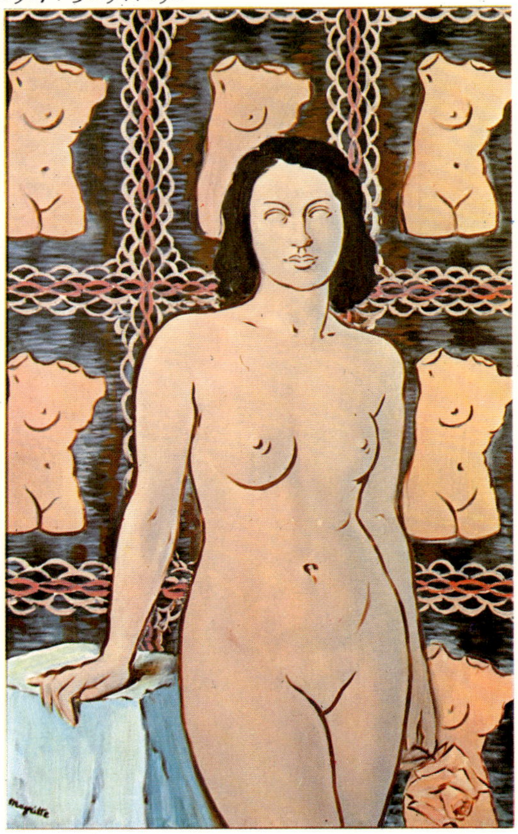

Lola de Valence
1948 / 38.6 × 23.6

of them had dared to open his eyes. The woman's very nakedness is a veil in the temple.

(1) *La philosophie dans le boudoir* (1948). The theme of living breasts on the hanging garment had already been used by Magritte in *In memoriam Mack Sennett,* in 1937.

(2) *La révolution surréaliste,* number 12, December 15, 1929.

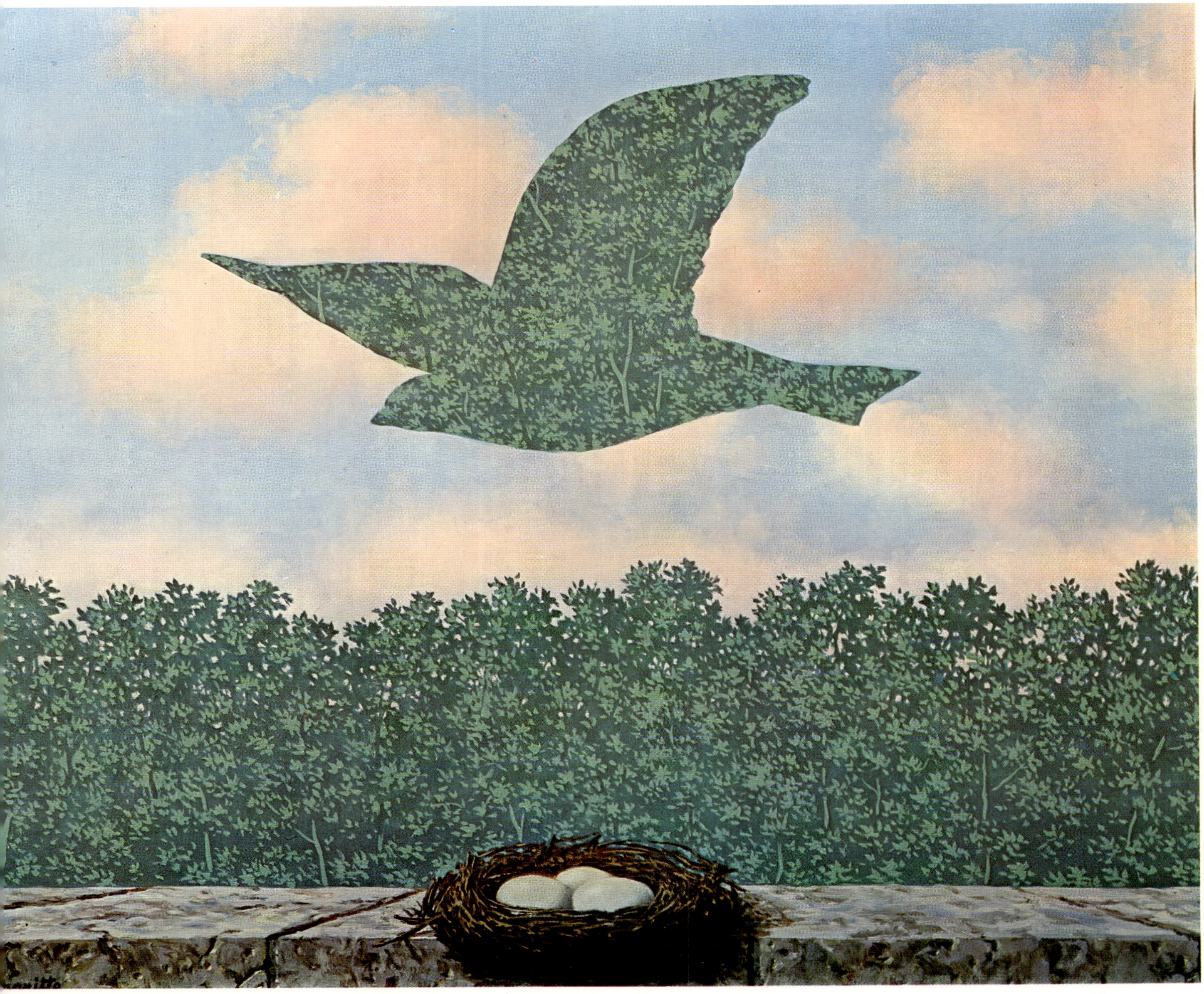

Spring (detail)
1965 / 18.1 × 24.6

The Sky
1943 / 11 4/5

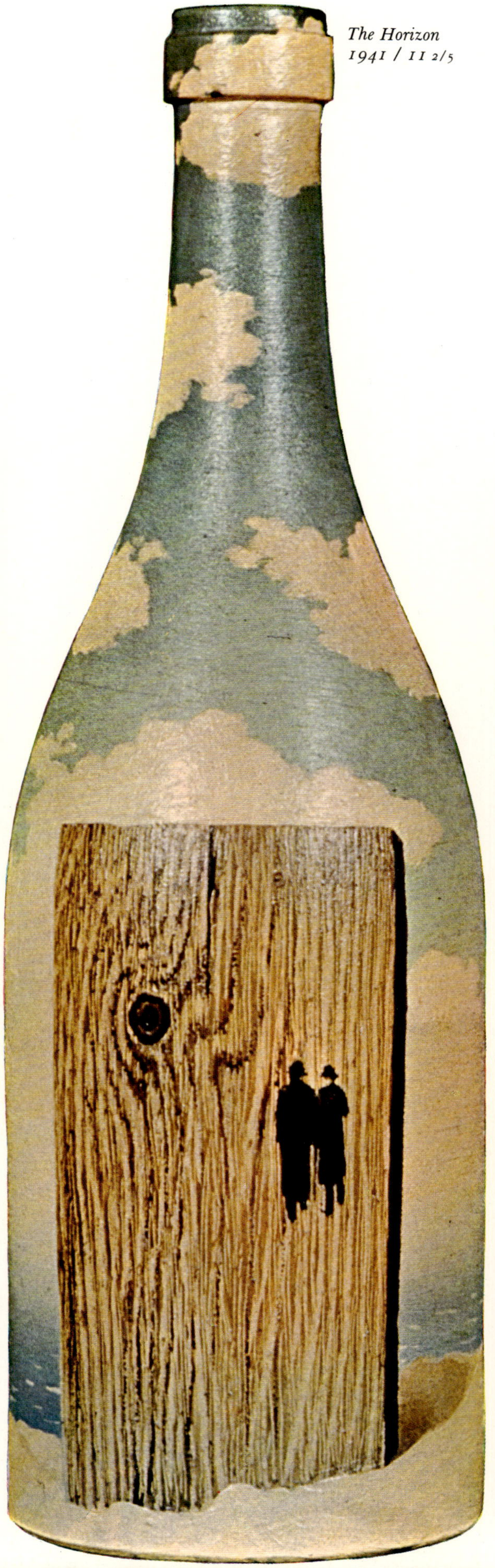

The Horizon
1941 / 11 2/5

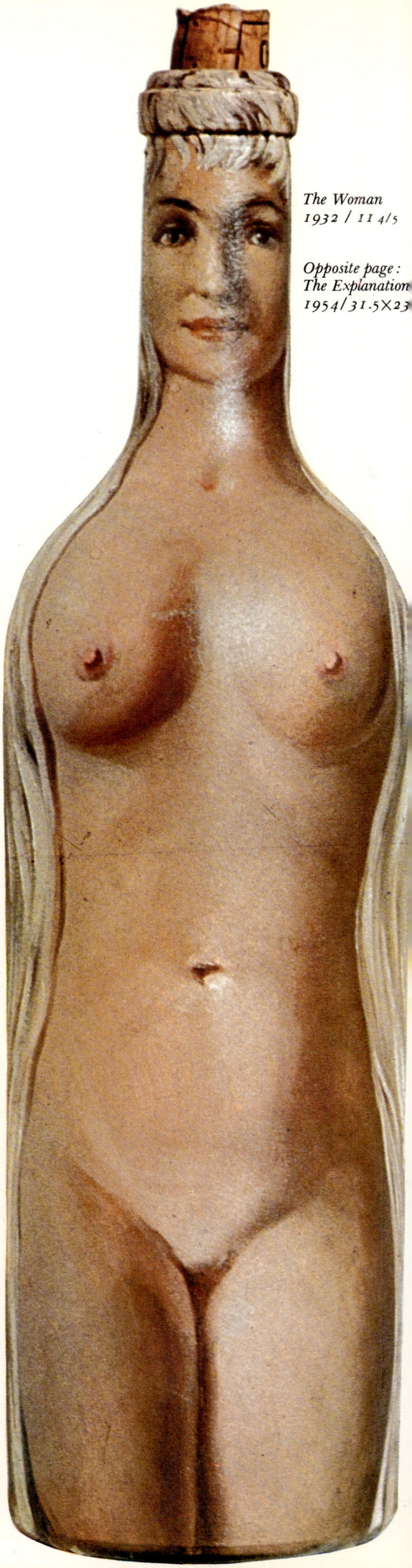

The Woman
1932 / 11 4/5

Opposite page:
The Explanation
1954/31.5×23

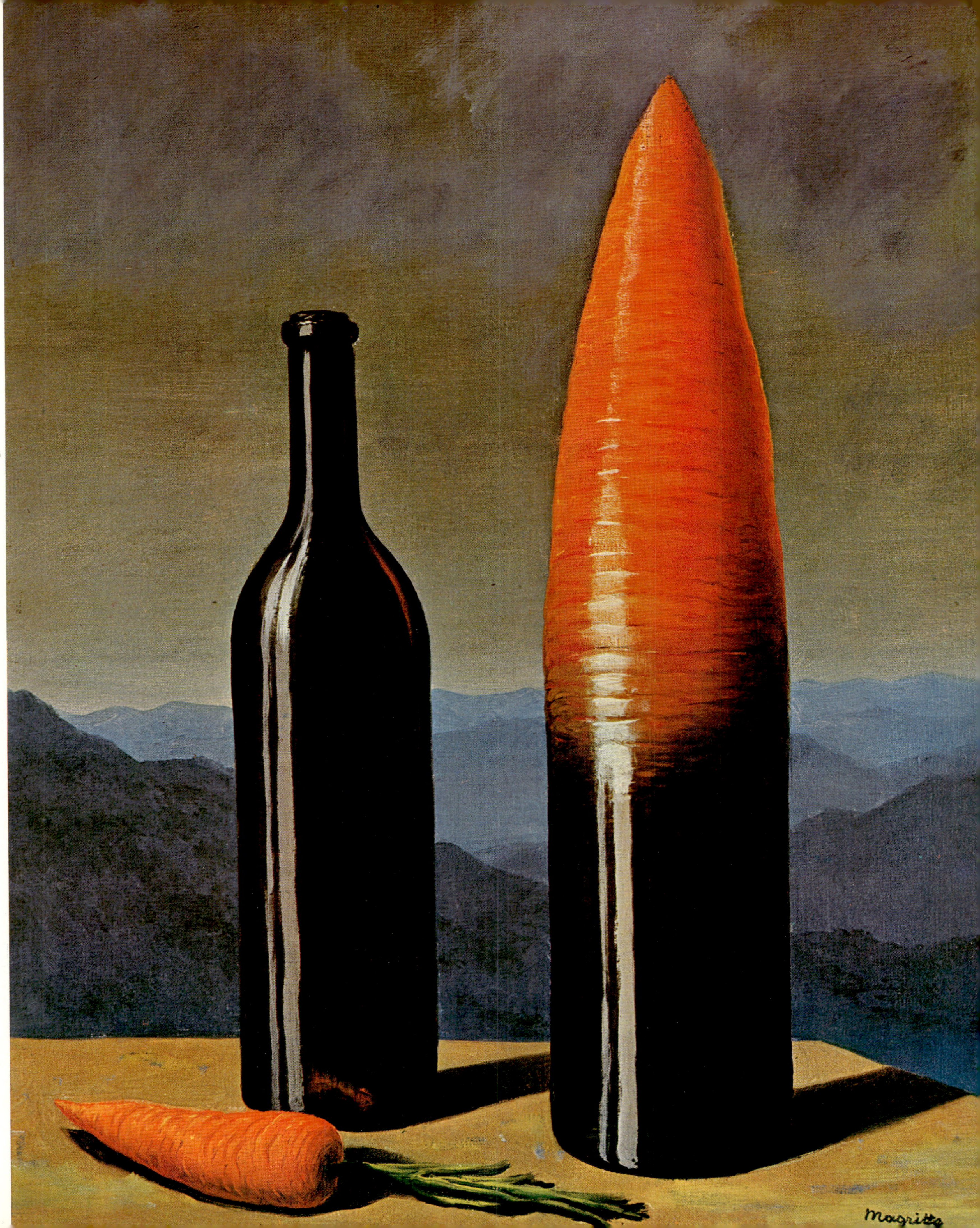
Magritte

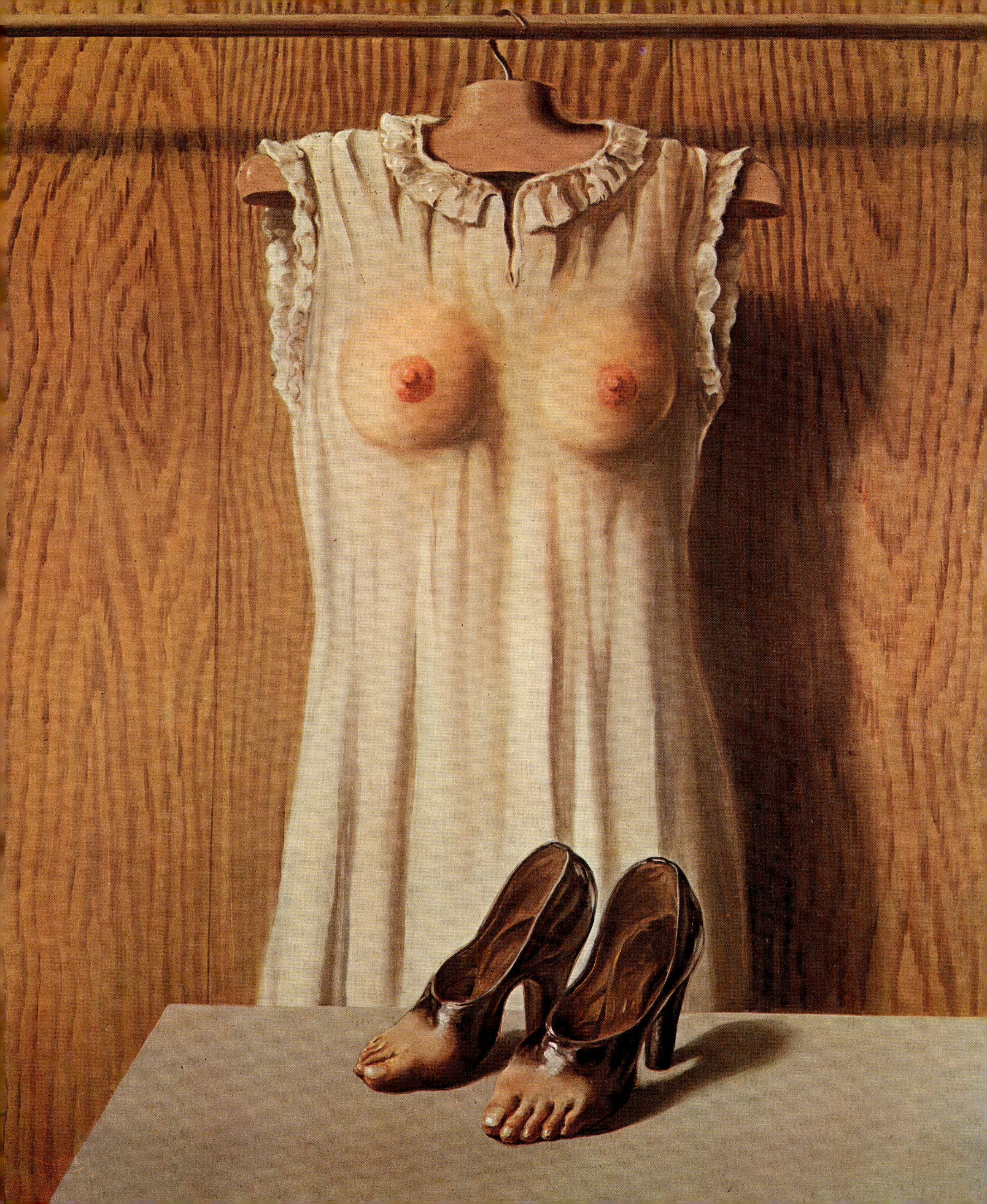

The Collective Invention
1954 / 31.8 × 44.5

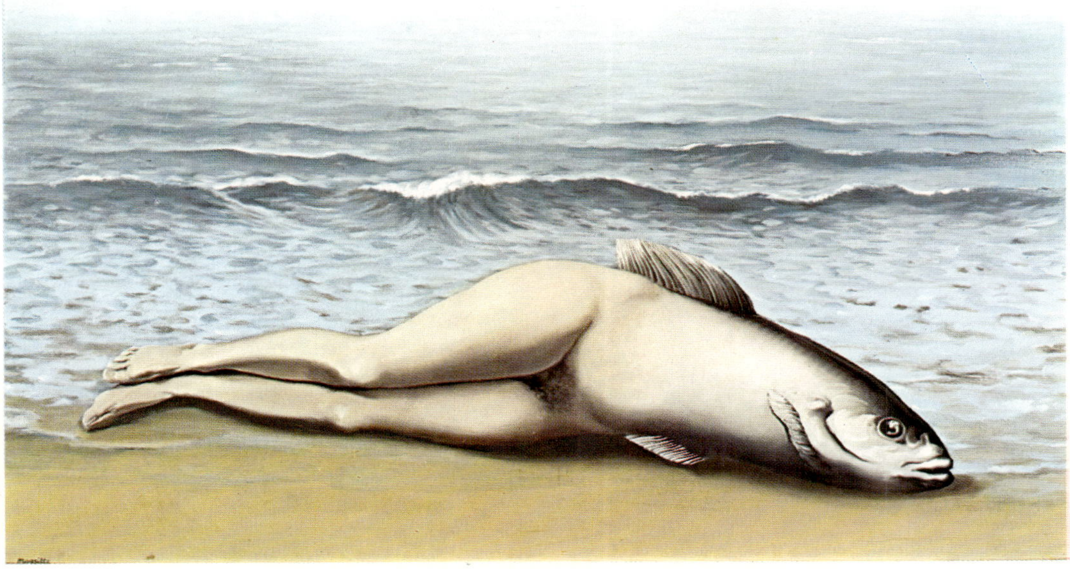

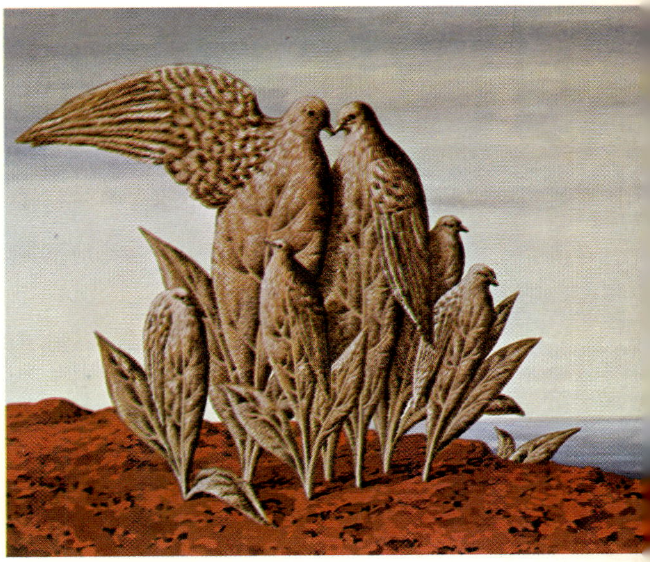

Treasure Island (detail)
Gouache 1937 / 13.4 × 19.6

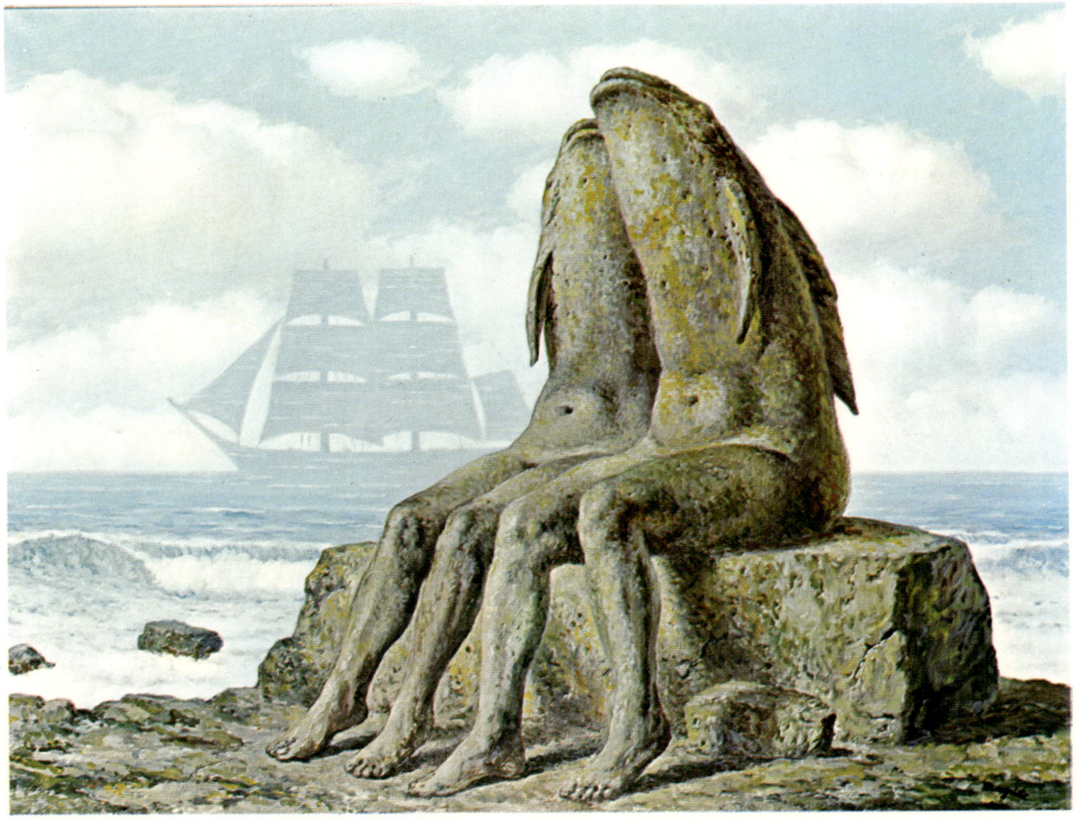

The Song of Love
1948 / 30.5 × 38.6

Opposite page:
Philosophy in the Boudoir
1947 / 31.9 × 24

Personal Values
1952 / 31.9 × 39.4

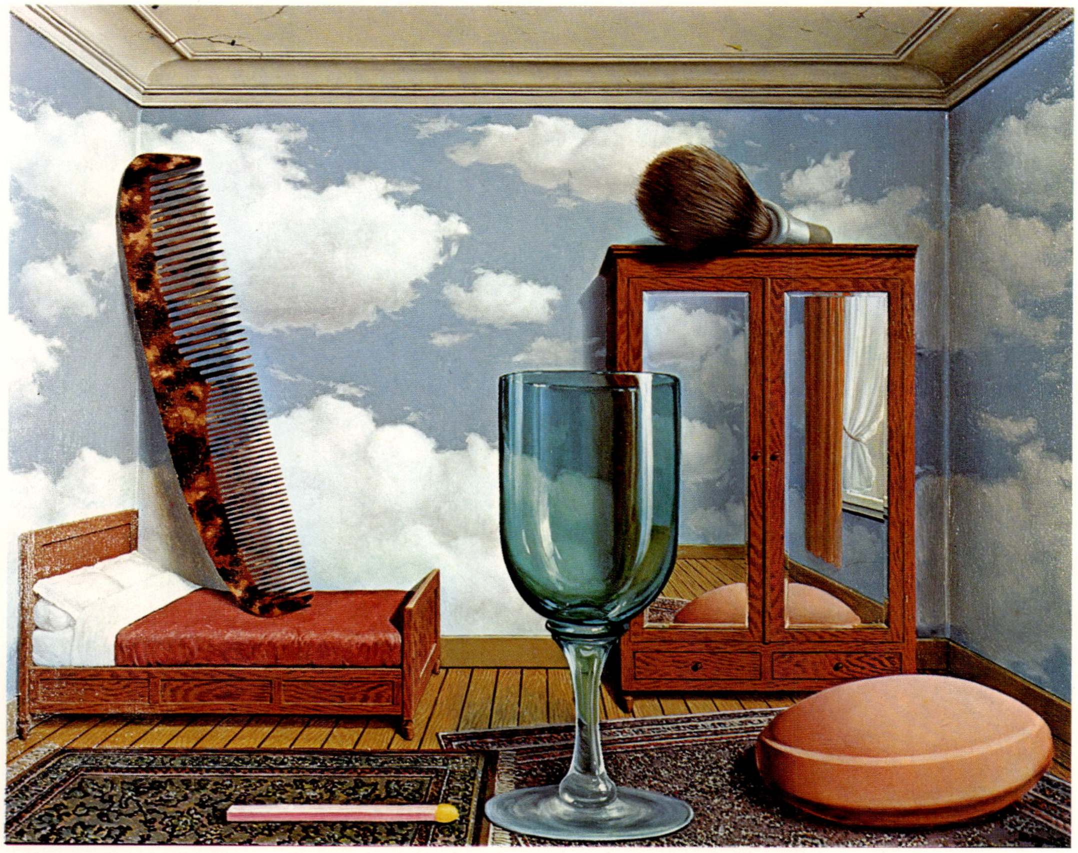

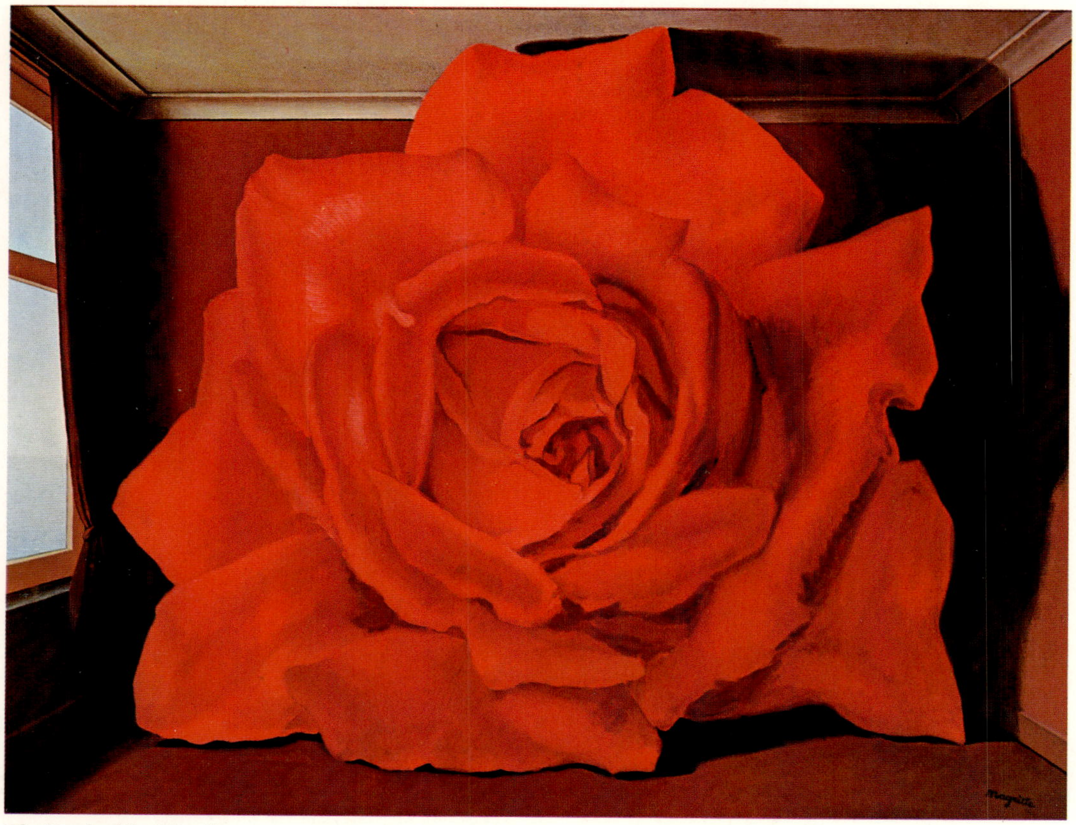

The Tomb of the Wrestlers
1960 / 35 × 46

Opposite page:
The Key of Dreams
1930 / 31.9 × 23.6

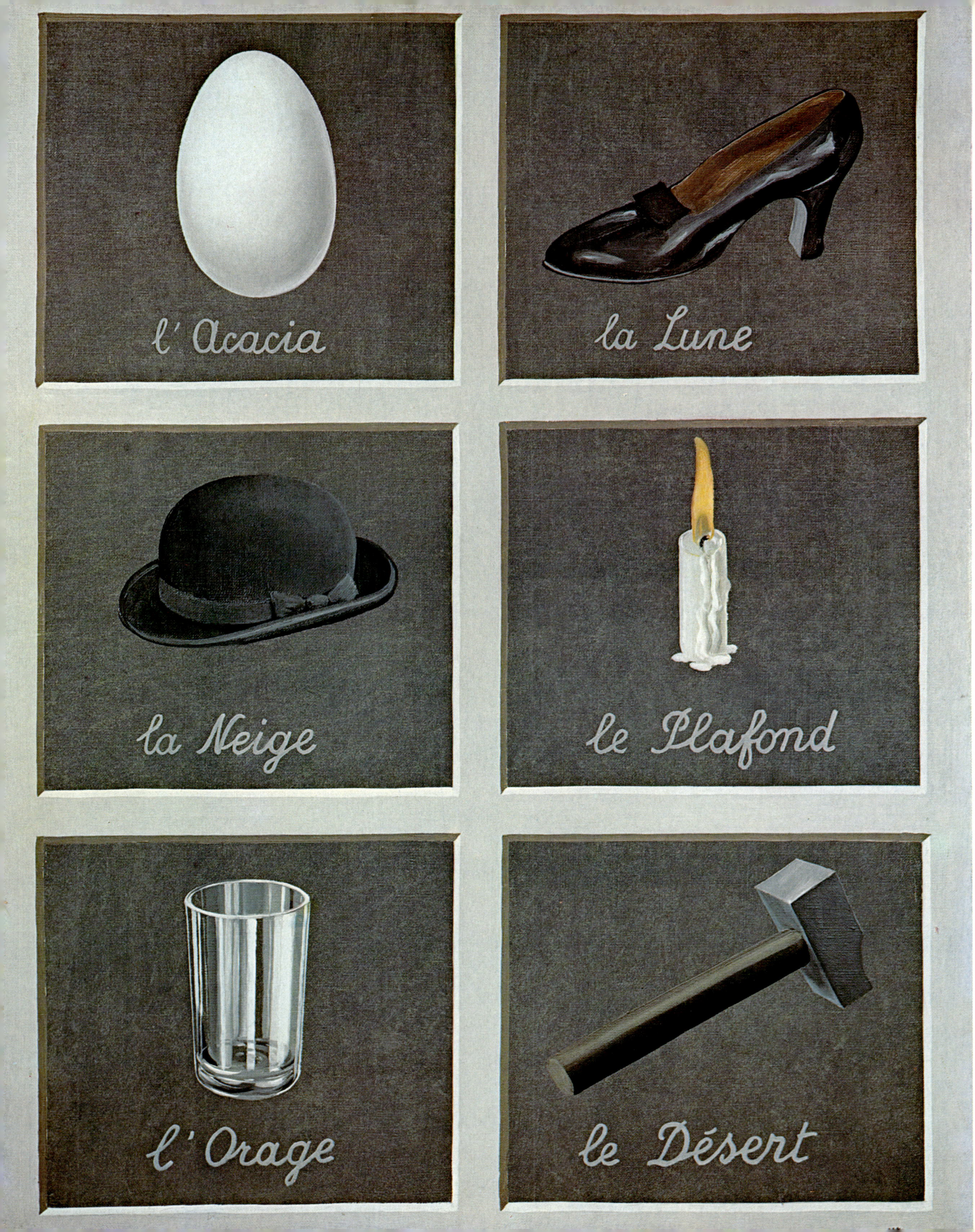
l'Acacia
la Lune
la Neige
le Plafond
l'Orage
le Désert

4 METAMORPHOSES AND SURREALISM

Nothing is certain,
but everything returns.
Everything points to another thing.
Everything whatever there
is treacherously removed.

Henri Michaux : *En rêvant à partir de peintures énigmatiques,* Mercure de France, December 1964, p. 597.

Like some great classical metaphysics, surrealism has attempted a derealization of things. This it did by two principal means, fluidification and uprooting. This is the thesis of M. Ferdinand Alquié in his *Philosophy of Surrealism*. (1).
"Sordid life" is transfigured by "admirable love." Jugs and apples, the human face and even woman's body are not interesting in themselves. One might say of reality what Breton said of painting that its "first care is to know what it leads to." (2). It must lead to the marvelous, which is beauty itself. *Explosante fixe, Magie circonstancielle* (3), what beauty turns up in the "light of the picture" where evidence of surrealism in conveyed by the irrepressible intervention of make believe. In consequence the surrealists achieve less a type of derealization (which would open on the Divine, the Beyond, the Great All, the Nothing) than a transfusion of subjectivity in objects obedient to man's inner power. They are convinced of the lack of reality in objects only in as much as they are left to their commercial, utilitarian and, let us say, unimaginative worries. But in the thrill of passionate love, which is poetry, they revive that reality and illumine it. Derealization then, in that sense. Transmutation of the real. How can Magritte deny reality, he who never ceases to nibble away at it? that a painting may be at the same time unrealistic and *chosiste* (to take over a word from Bachelard), that is what makes undeniable the existence of that "state of mind in which life and death, the real and the imaginary, the past and the future, the communicable and the uncommunicable, the high and the low, cease to be perceived as contradictory." (4).
With Magritte, derealization passes through a metamorphosis that is less a marvelous transfiguration than a cold victory of irony.
No fluidity, no drippings, as in Dali, fairly little viscosity. Uprooting, yes, which is a sort of metamorphosis of places. A woman's torso, a trombone and a chair appear in a cloudless sky: it is *le Temps menaçant* (1928). Familiar objects are placed against a hazy sky (*les Valeurs personnelles,* 1952). A rose has unfolded until it fills the room. The dum-bell and the sportsman's head are superimposed to such an extent in *Mouvement perpétuel* (1934) that our halting gaze seems to enter that head and that ball endlessly – only a smile draws us way.

Is it uprooting or metamorphosis? A game played by Magritte has to do with the name of objects, the game of denying names. Of an apple, especially an apple, one says: "This is not an apple."
The same with a pipe. To be sure we could not eat that apple which is only a painted image, nor smoke that pipe. (5). Sometimes an empty form with vague outlines pierces a design, but a few words are written on it: "gun," or "person bursting with laughter." The word creates the objects which, however, does not go so far as to become visible, remaining half-way between being and nothingness. Elsewhere three naked women become signs when on each of them is written the meaning that Magritte alone has the power to give them: "tree, projecting shadow, wall." The written language intervenes on the graphic image, literally bursts into it to fix its meaning despite what our eyes have already named it. Though not more literary than others, Magritte's painting is always enriched by that intrusion of the word, of which the titles given to pictures are only a particular mode of intervention. The success of these verbal windfalls makes one think of one of those surrealist games, where chance is mingled with poetic impulses: the acacia is an egg, a woman's shoe is called the moon, the desert is a hammer. In such examples the image lives only through its legend: the written word carries its meaning with it, just as the pictured image evokes the word that designates it. Then egg and acacia become merged in our mind... a metamorphosis one might consider reached by a lazy method if plastic means were still possible.

Here are some metamorphoses that are completely represented by the picture. They are sometimes caught in the act of being born. An eagle's head is about to produce a rocky peak... The erotic eye makes toes appear in the slippers and breasts on the gown: a magic operation is in progress. Leaves are still turning into birds... But rape has been done. The most effective shock-pictures bring us up short before the ultimate immobility, as final, as definitive, as the metamorphoses. The bottle is transformed into a woman (anyone who can pick up a litre in both hands then seizes an available waist). In more trivial fashion the same bottle can end by being a carrot.
And we note that many of Magritte's metamorphoses are in the vertical sense of his instinct for ridicule. A nose in the bowl of a pipe, becomes long, obscene. Medieval towers end in being soft snakes. In the moonlight, two apples wear masks to hide their lack of vision. The siren, whom tradition calls a mermaid, a woman-fish (ending in fish below, which plunges us into animalism) becomes a fish-woman, stranded on the beach: her green pollack head is apparently unable to shake off the inertia of her body and her legs. And yet, a couple of those monsters, seated on a stone, appear to be exchanging gossipy confidences... In several canvases dealing with the same them *(les Grâces naturelles, les Compagnons de la Peur)* birds take root and become plants. The

tree itself, duly planted in the ground, becomes an enormous leaf: the whole is reduced to the part, the durable strength of a tree-trunk to the frailty of a leaf-stalk. Or else a trunk with dry roots, in mid-sky, changes into a ruined dungeon. The head of the murderer (of the *vache* period) is distorted into shadowy chicks. The guitar gets caught in a face.

All the metamorphoses of matter (if one may call it that) are affected by vertical decline. The tree is brick, old wall; the bird in full flight is only jagged branches or worse – thick clay. A whole part of Magritte's works transforms objects into that ridiculous material sculptors use as modeling paste. Apple on a pedestal, fruit dish,

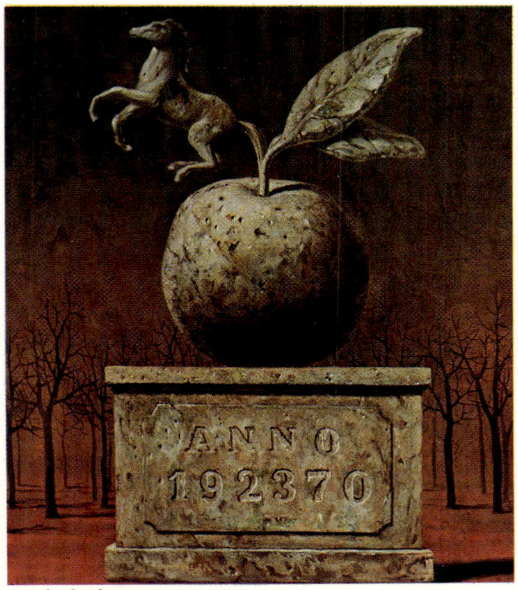

Smoked Glasses
1951 / 22.6 × 19.1

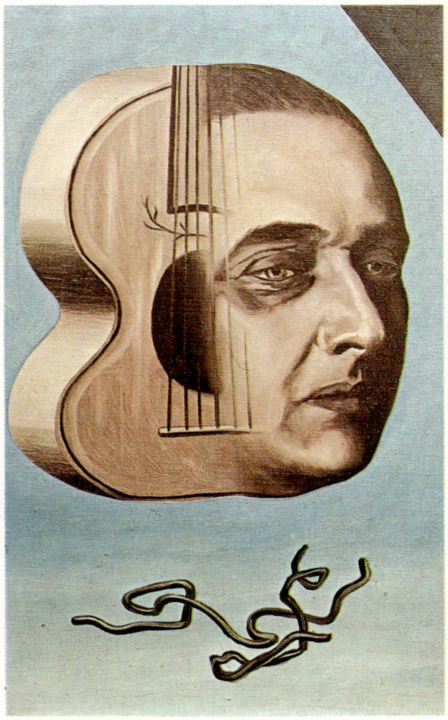
P.G. Van Hecke (detail)
1927 / 24 × 19.3

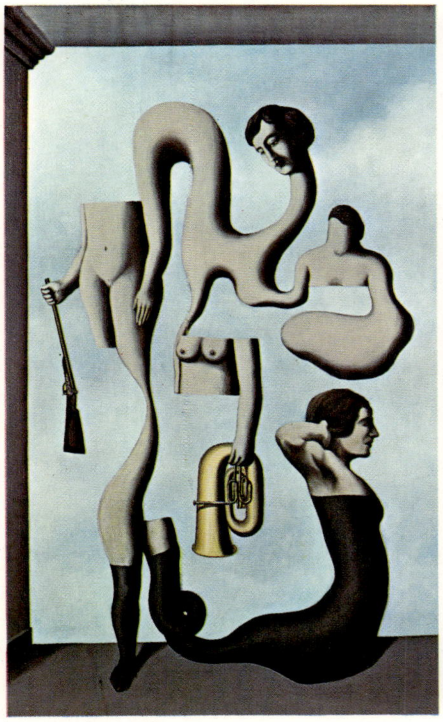
The Acrobat's Ideas
1928 / 45.6 × 31.9

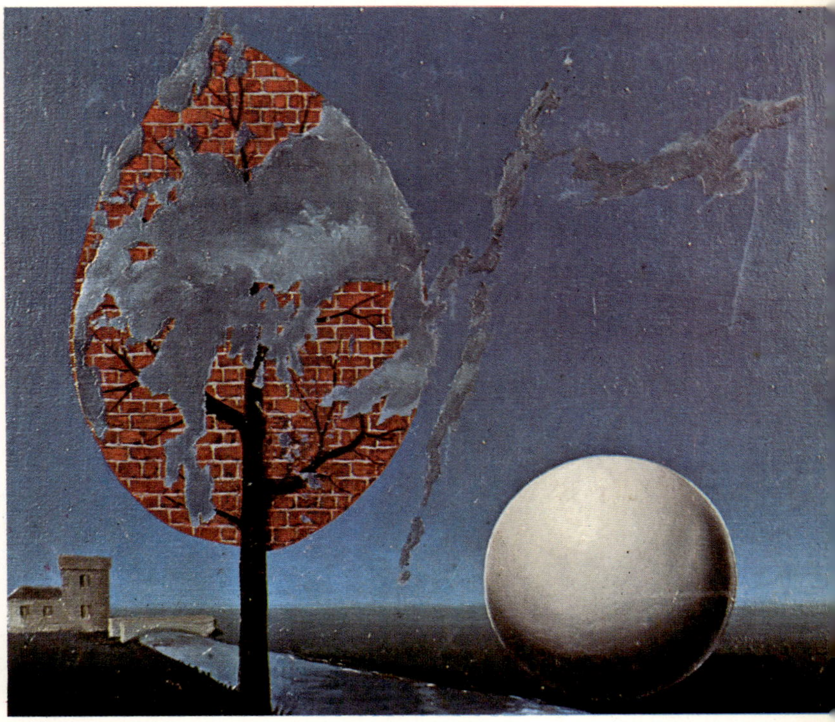
Passion Flower
1936 / 17.8 × 21.6

bird... The most astonishing thing is those two gentlemen in hats and long overcoats, one of whom, in a gesture we would call fraternal, cuts out the eye of the other man who lets him do it even more submissively than the woman in the *Chien andalou*. The scene, treated as trompe-l'œil, looks like the photograph of a bas-relief in terra cotta. Entitled *Journal intime*, we find in it several of Magritte's outstanding themes: the theme of the double, the punishment of the eye, petrification. Nothing is more stifling than that mutation into clay. Even when cold, painting which always usés a little color, is repudiated, scoffed at by the wand of this magician who transfixes it. The same one, who seemed to open space to great distances of cold, is filled with a dream of solid material, heavy, rendered inert, a dead material. One of the keys to Magritte's deep-seated pessimism lies in pictures like these which show this painter to be far removed from the sunny and lyrical surrealism of André Breton. To paint sculpture faithfully adds perhaps a joke, but on the occasion of this absurdity, we witness a sinister triumph of matter.

Magritte does not bring about a magic derealization of the world; on the contrary, he reifies it in sadness. Alone with his gloom (in spite of his period known as "full sunlight"), he leans, to the point of nausea, over the pit of viscosity he has finally accepted.

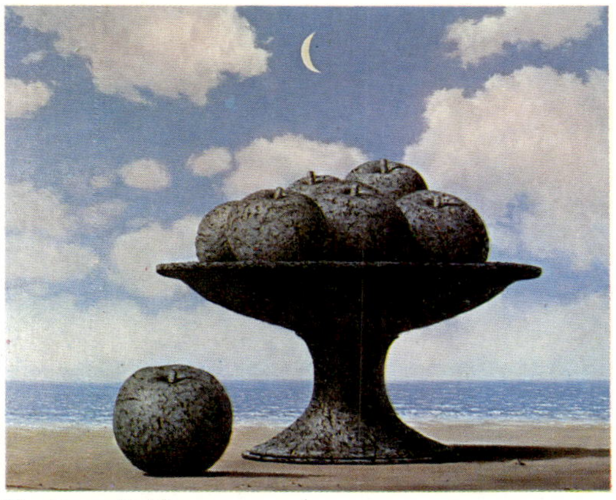
The Large Table
Without date / 20.9 × 24.8

(1) Paris, Flammarion, 1955; Ann Arbor, University of Michigan Press, 1965.
(2) *Le surréalisme et la peinture*. First part.
(3) *L'Amour fou*. Paris, Gallimard, 1937, p. 26.
(4) Second Manifesto of Surrealism, 1929.
(5) Michel Foucault enumerates seven significant connections possible in "This is not a pipe." See, *Ceci n'est pas une pipe*. Cahiers du chemin, Paris, Gallimard, 1968, p. 75-105.

Dangerous Acquaintances
1936 / 28.3 × 25.2

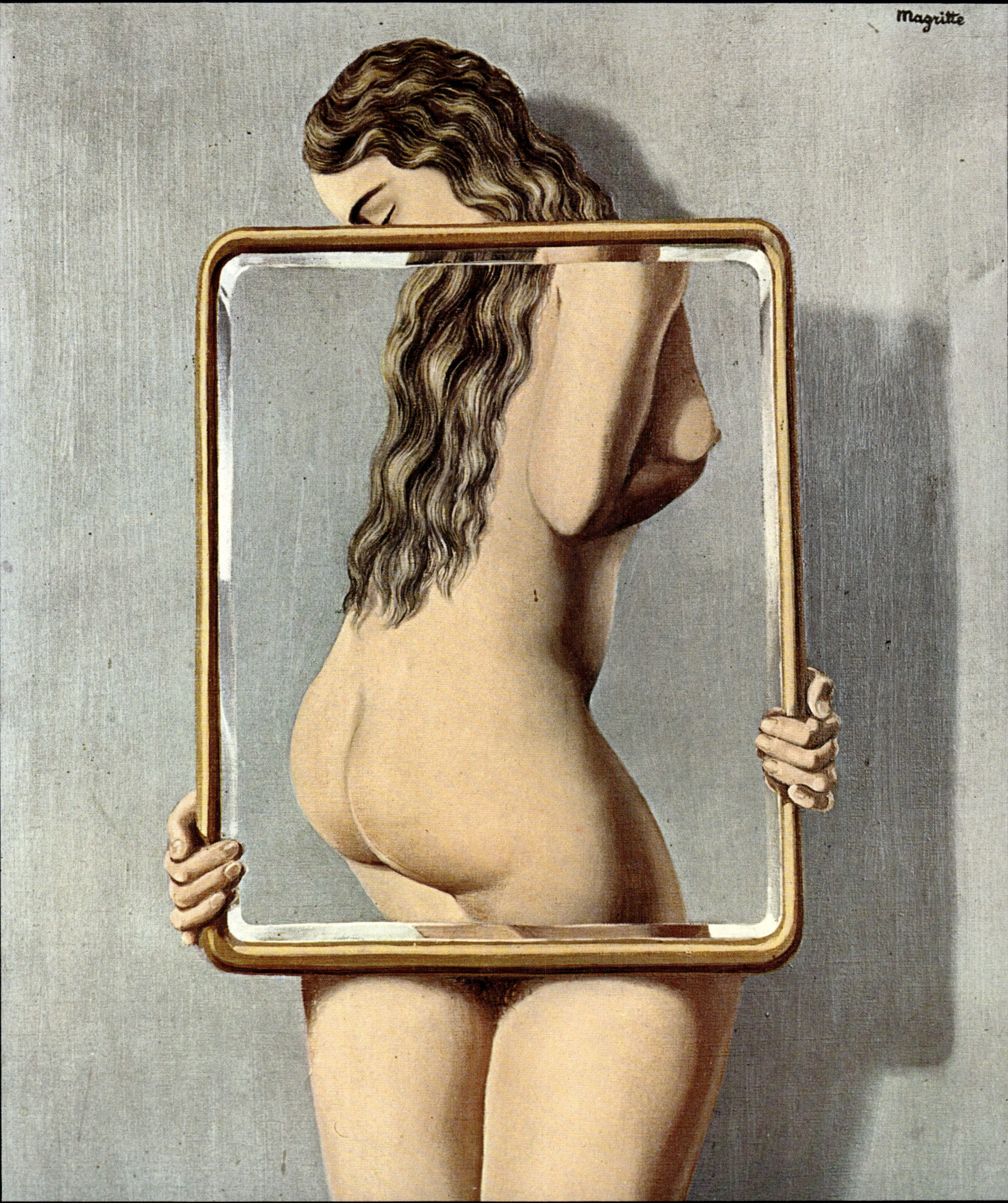

5. THE LAWS OF THE ABSURD

Tortures of the Vestal
1926 / 37.4 × 28.8

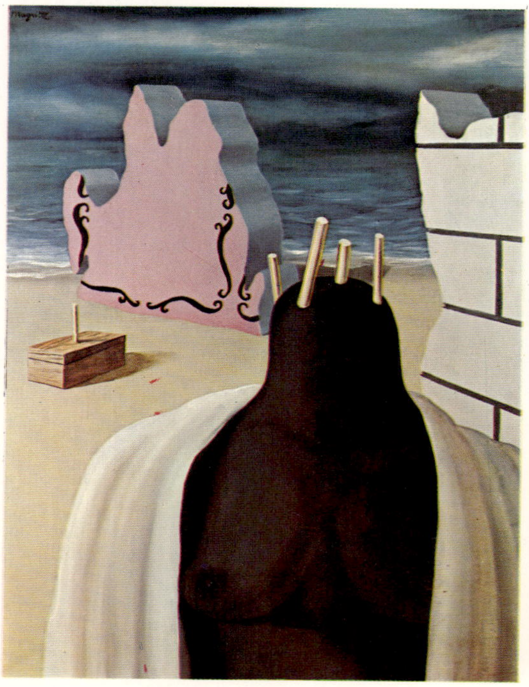

The Man of the Sea
1926 / 55.1 × 43.3

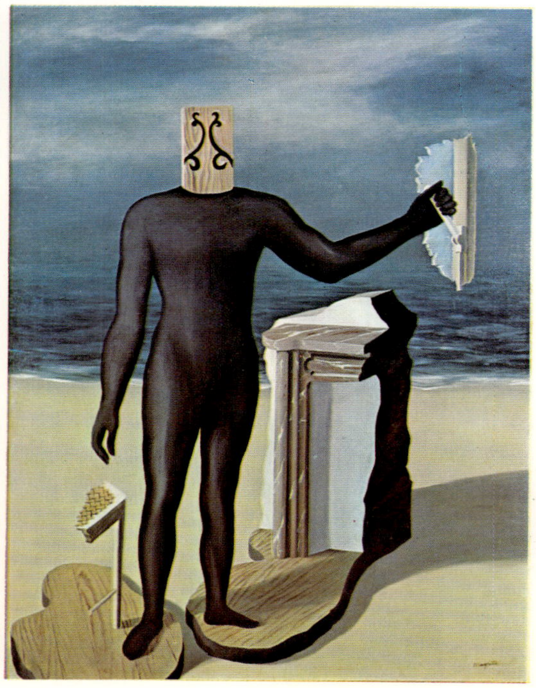

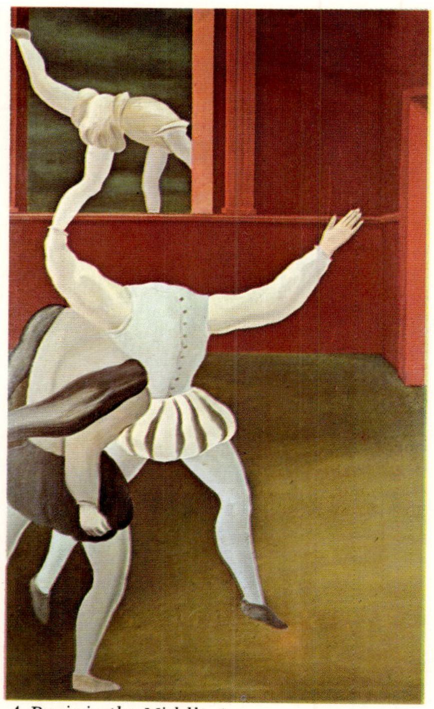

A Panic in the Middle Ages
1927 / 38.6 × 29.1

Opposite page:
The Liberator
1947 / 38.6 × 30.7

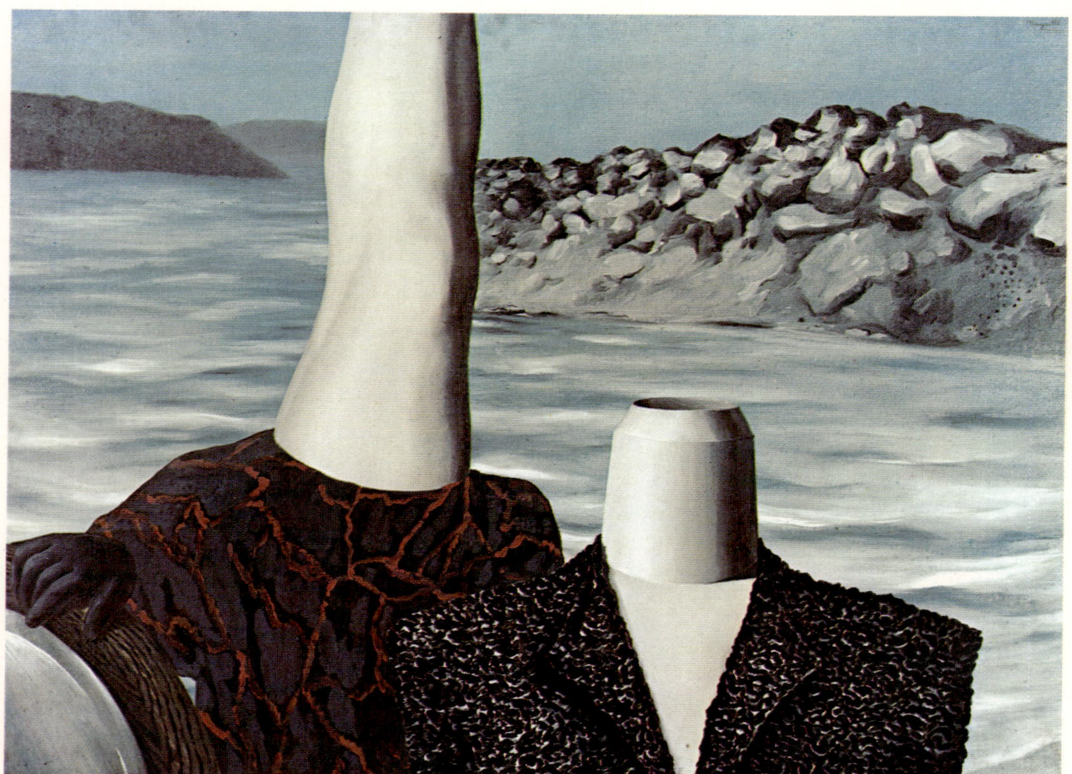

The Inhabitants of the River
1926 / 29.1 × 38.6

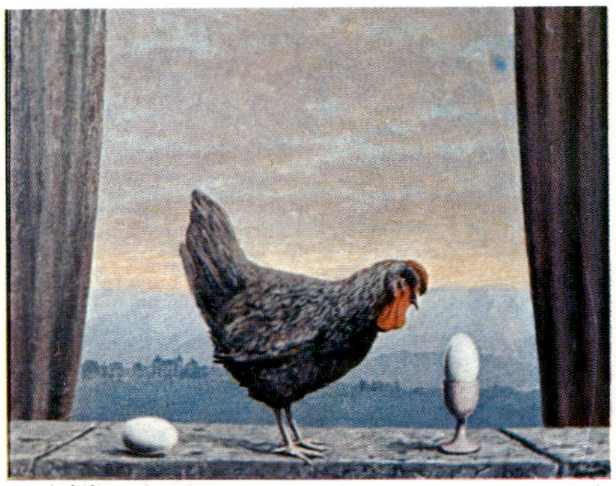
Variability of Sadness
1955 / 19.6 × 23.6

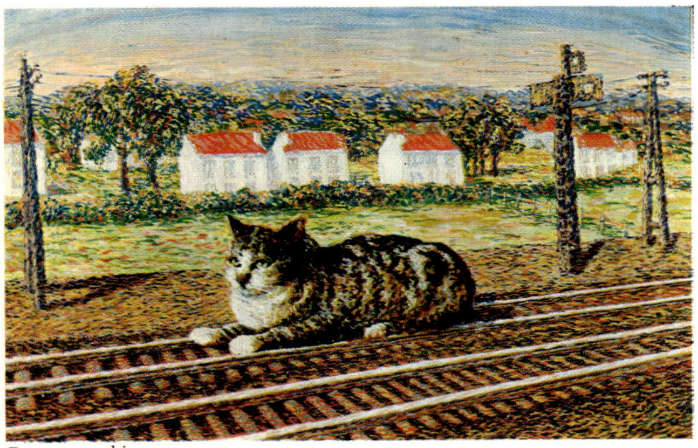
Ramnagrobis
Gouache 1948 / 24 × 16.8

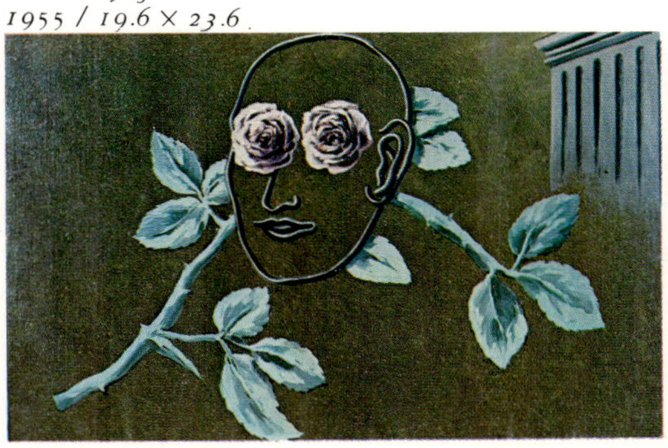
The Voyage of the Flowers
1928 / 28.8 × 35.4

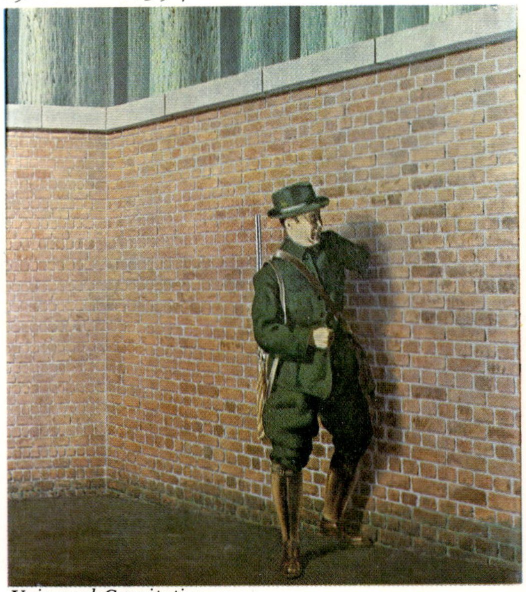
Universal Gravitation
1943 / 39.4 × 28.8

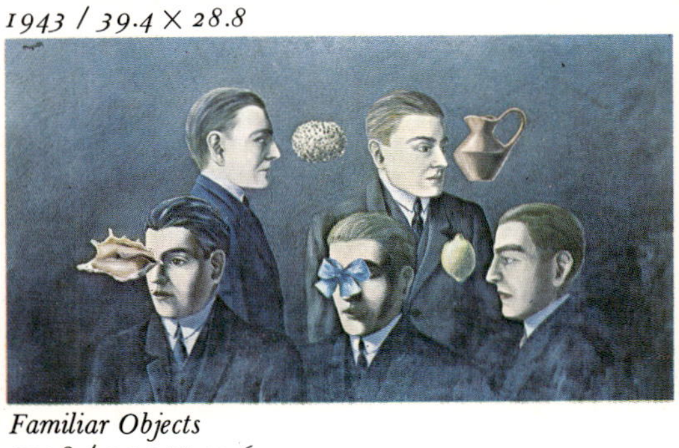
Familiar Objects
1928 / 31.9 × 45.6

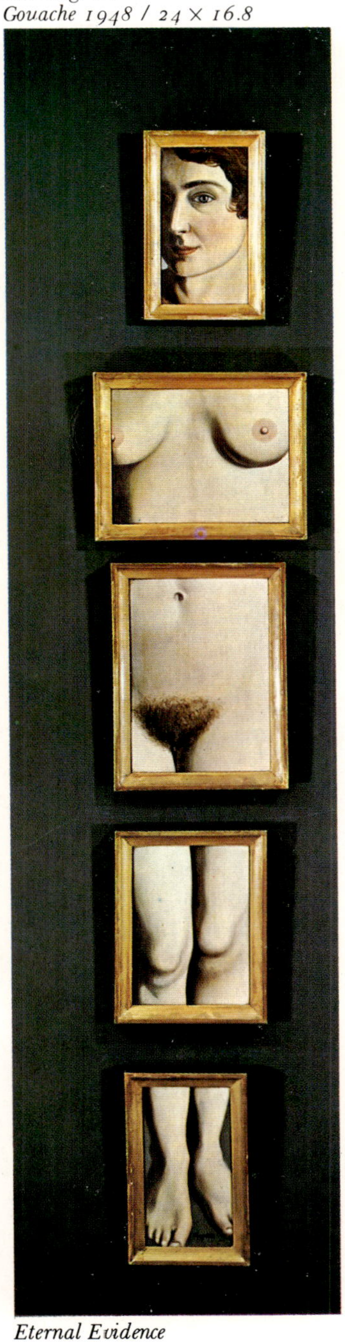
Eternal Evidence
(Five canvases) 1930 /
8.6 × 4.8, 7.1 × 9,
10.4 × 7.3, 8.5 × 6.1,
8.5 × 4.5

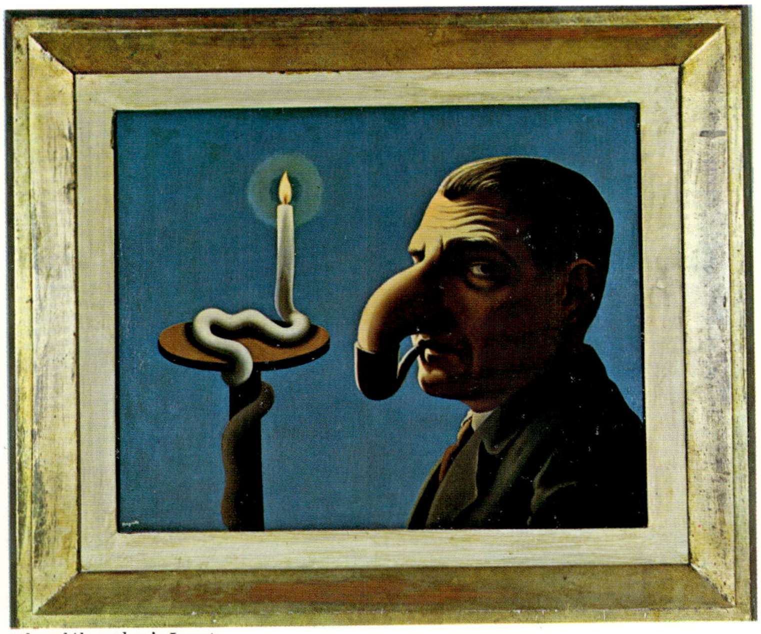
The Philosopher's Lamp
1936 / 17.7 × 25.2

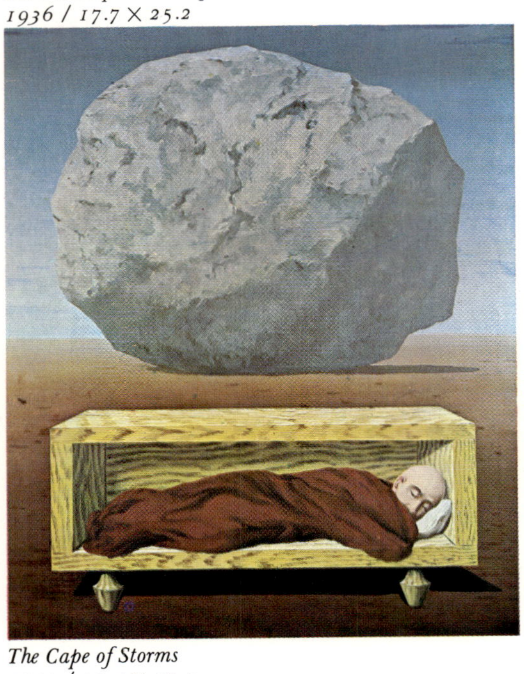
The Cape of Storms
1945 / 39.4 × 31.9

Revelation of the Present
1936 / 18.1 × 25.6

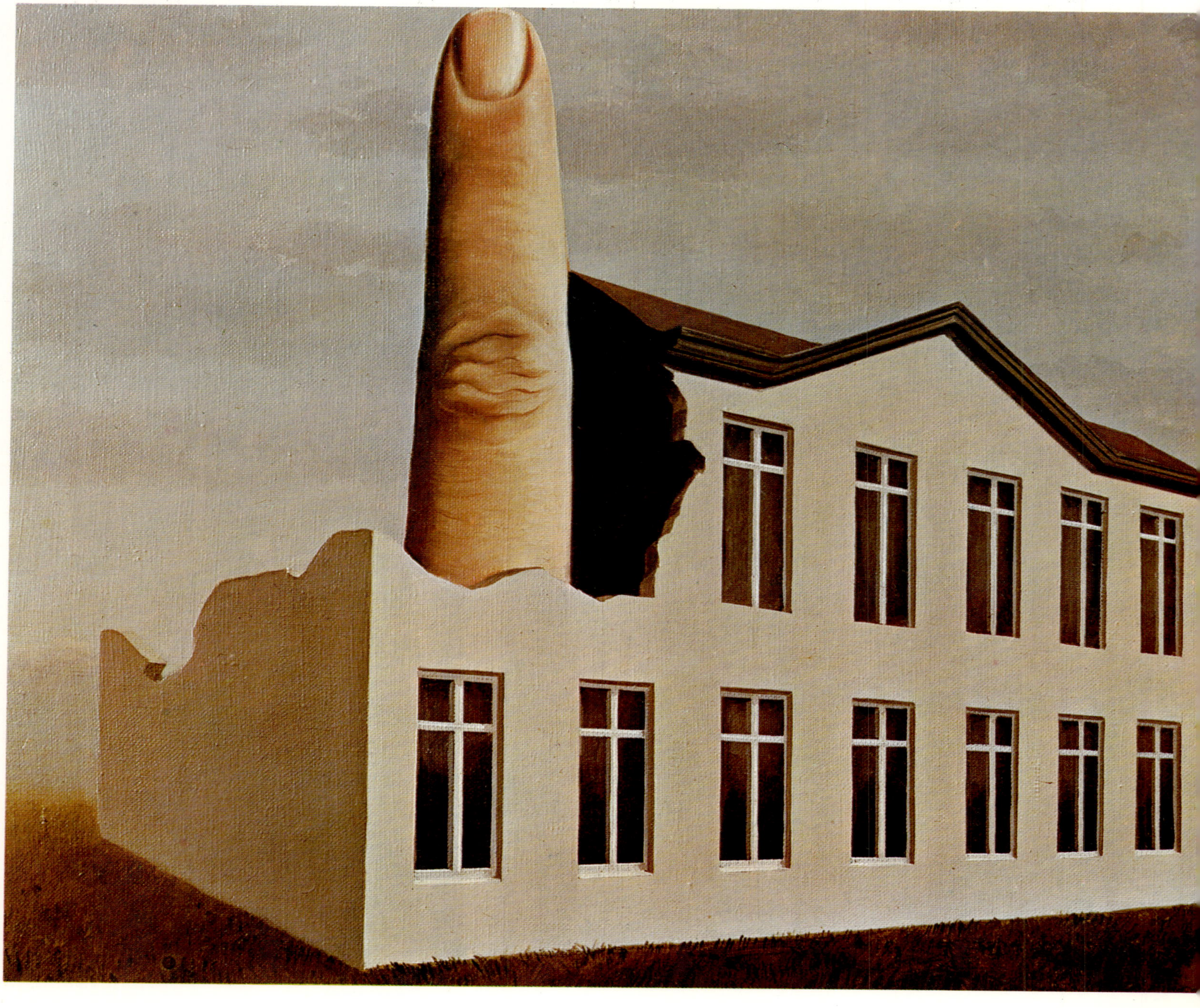

Natural Encounters
1945 / 31.5 × 25.6

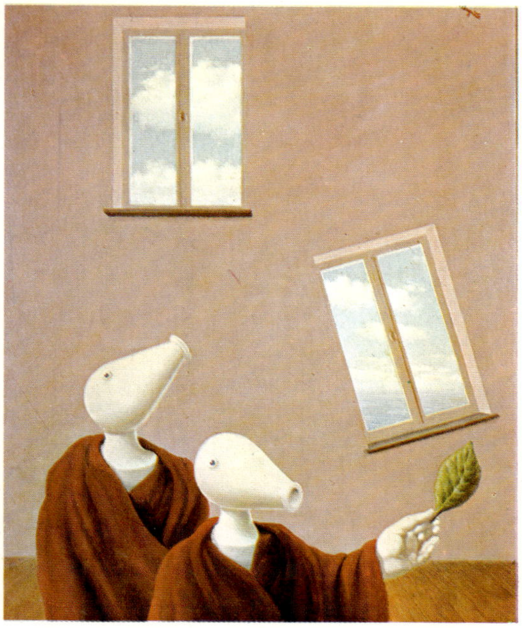

Mental Look
Gouache without date / 20.9 × 13.8

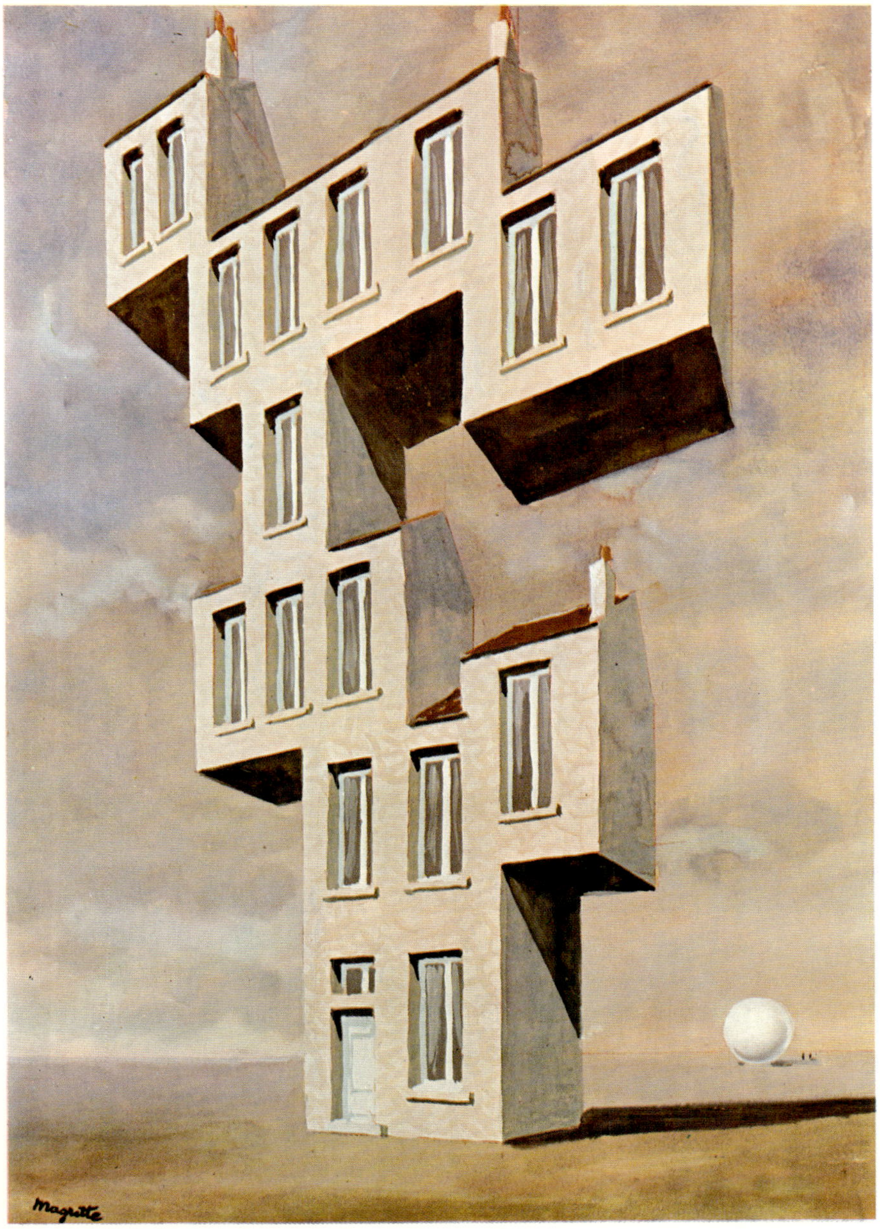

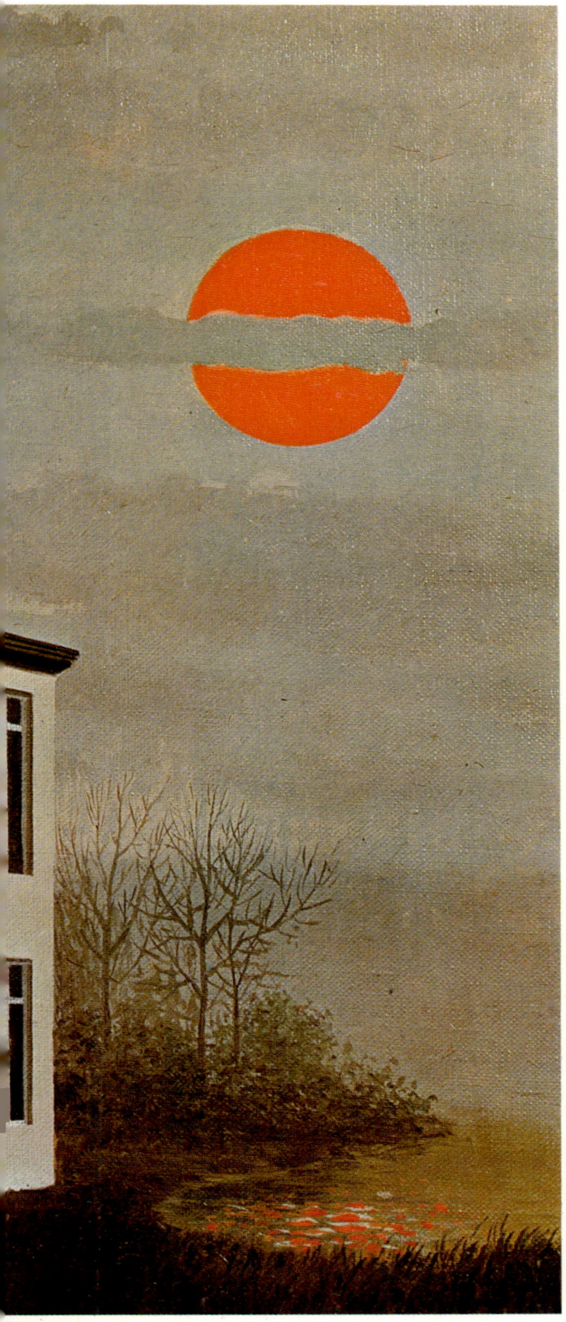

Following pages:
The Bosom
1960 / 20 × 27.6

Below:
The Use of the Word
1934-1935 / 21.2 × 28.8

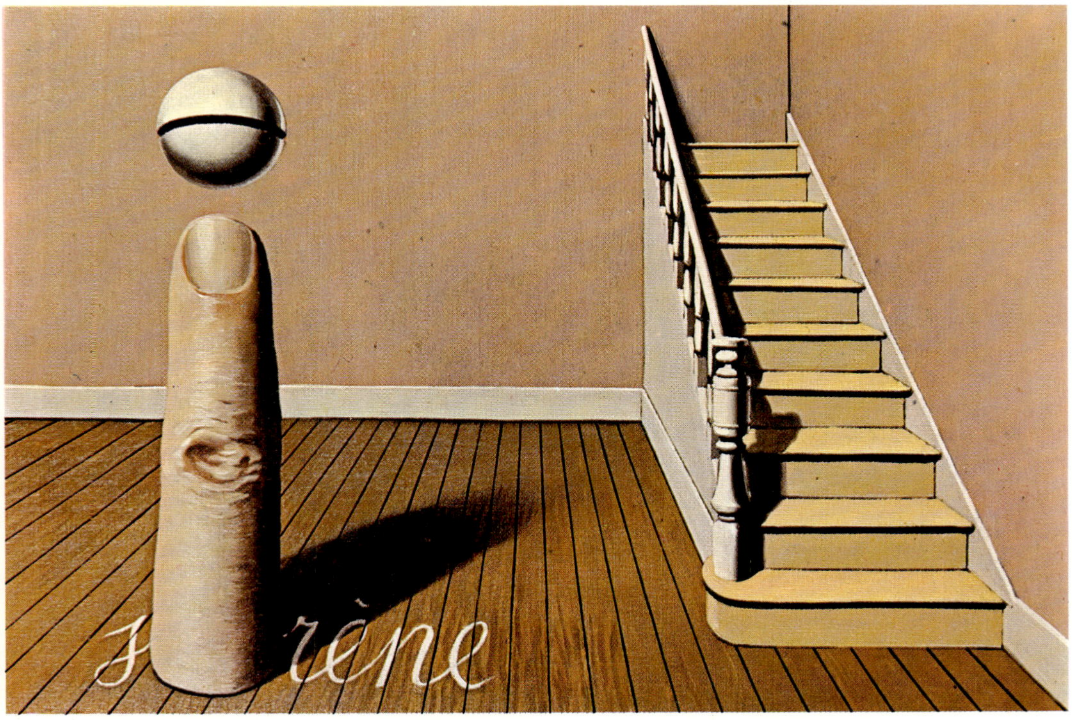

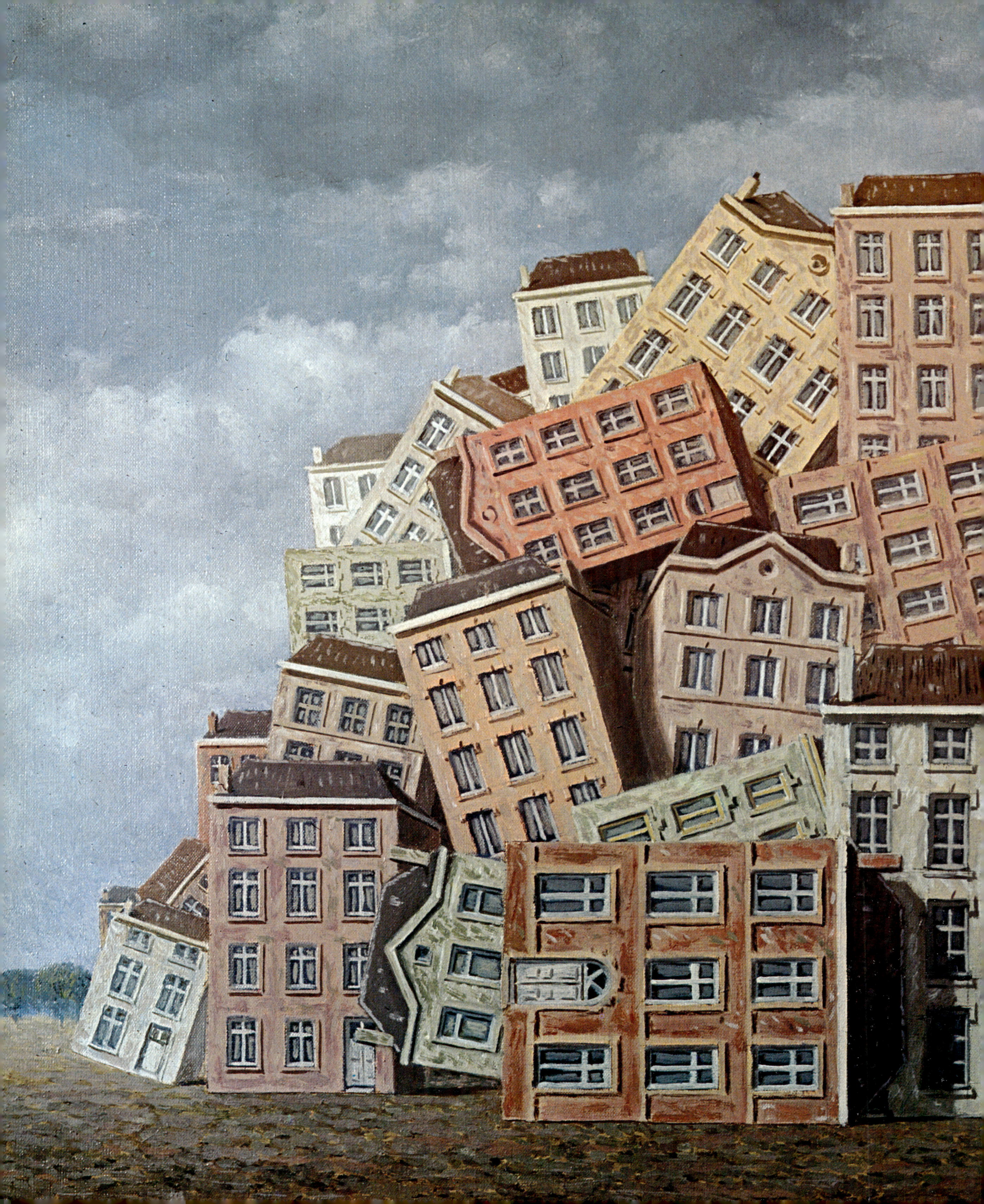

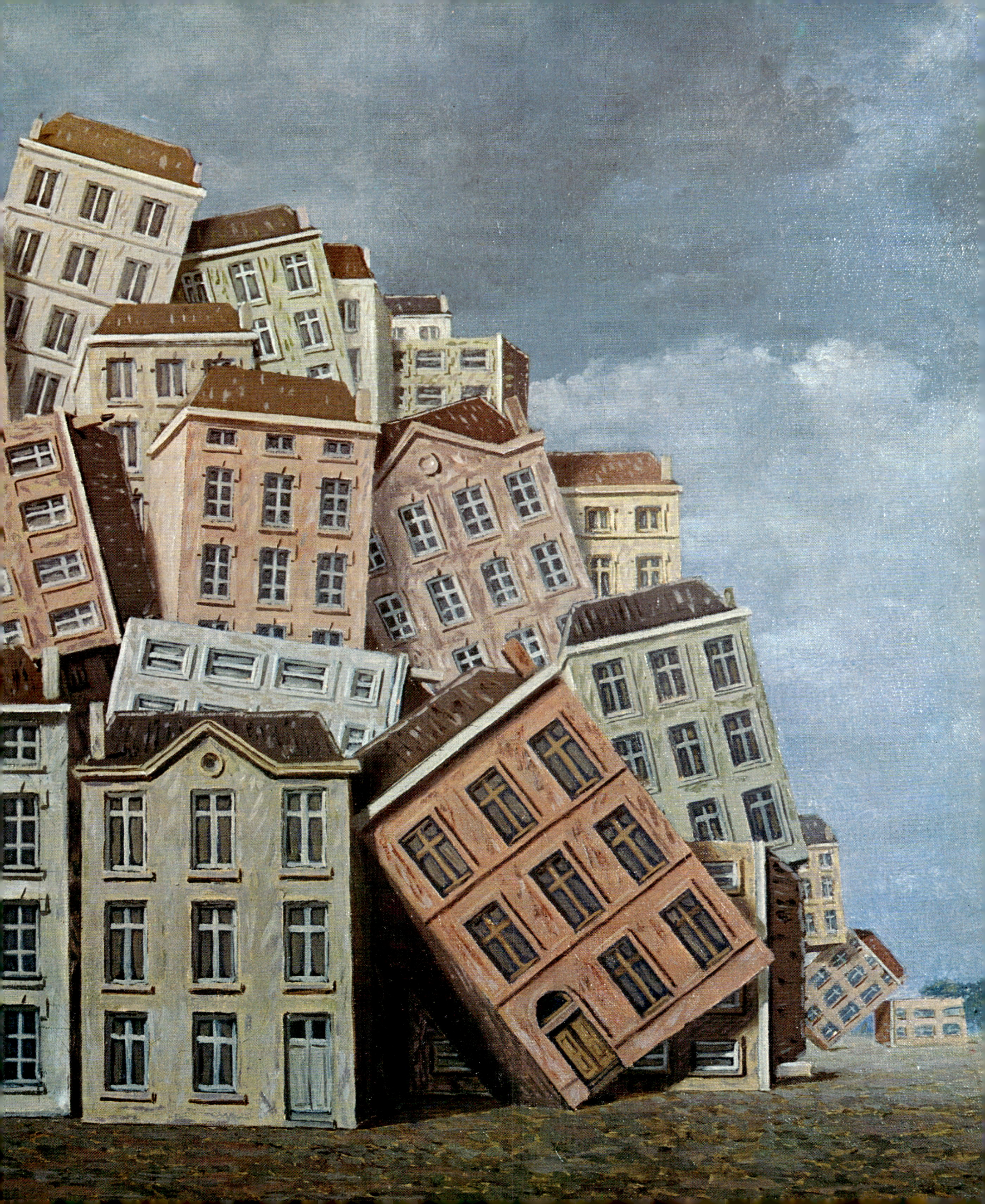

5 THE LAWS OF THE ABSURD

Art is "the creation of a sensitive reality modifying the world in response to the desire for wonders, which is part of the essence of the human being." (Georges Bataille, *Lascaux*, Geneva, Skira, 1955. Quoted by Patrick Waldberg in *Magritte*).

What does it matter to us that Magritte sometimes amused himself with the nature of things? From broad comedy to the treasures of humor his delight in play never excludes a primordial gravity, a sort of intellectual sadness. And if, by being multiplied, the metamorphoses, the challenges to the logic of space, reach a sort of delirium, it is because, with Magritte, human reason cannot resign itself to that "mystery of the world" which philosophers term the absurd. It protests, but never loses hope. The world has no meaning. Less than an enigma, less than a mystery, inexplicable as long as we do not have the key to it, the world is the absolute non-sense. "Why is there something rather than nothing?" (1) asks Heidegger. Why that particular being rather than another? For no reason at all. Then don't try to fool us with the order of things, the harmonies of nature, physical theory, psychoanalysis, structure! To the fundamental absurdities of the world, Magritte hurls back the absurdities by which the freedom of motion, the freedom to laugh, to love, to paint, make a hole in our solid and stifling existence. Weight, perspective, the upright position, feminine beauty, bourgeois respectability, all that is put in the same sack with due allowance for the absurdity of the essential thing, the right to laugh at it.

It is therefore irony in Magritte, irony as a higher form of conscience that is clothed in humor, the sense of the fundamentally absurd that is prolonged, not without aggressiveness, in more or less knowledgeable doses, in more or less regular laws, in this game that is really a struggle. To establish the rules of that struggle would be to risk turning into prescriptions what, in Magritte, rises from a spiritual technique. We shall mention only a few major methodes.

I. Physical Contradiction. Not only does he put nature at variance with itself, but he adds contradiction to it. Under all possible angles. He enflames the non-combustible metal of a musical instrument. He wakens life in rocks, the animal in the vegetable. The stump of a tree that has been cut down, raises one of its roots like an arm and seizes the hatchet. Visual screens are disturbed. The rider on her horse rides through the underbrush. The open door in the *Enfant retrouvé* (1966) (2) shows an interior setting in which a few trees appear. Weight is denied. A piece of rock is suspended in the sky, a castle is even set on it. The heavier the stone (all the pictorial effects tend to make it weighty) the dizzier is its levitation. There is no longer even the beautiful simplicity of gravity; it is the inner contradiction of the heavy-lightened. The negative mass. Unthinkable! The bird petrified in clay, but which nevertheless flies, the men, sowing or talking together, in the sky, the loaves of bread that sail past like clouds, all that is making game of Newton and Einstein. Absurd in its very being, the world is absurdly disorganized in its laws.

II. The logical blending. Magritte, however, plays a more subtle game in which the simplicities of contradiction yield to relations of mental proximity. Despite their differences in order, realm or usage, things sometimes have affinities among themselves in which logic is involved. Magritte penetrates the secret association of objects, some of which pose questions and others furnish replies. (3). *Les Affinités électives* (1933) substitutes the egg for the bird in the cage. It is not a natural contradiction, but an absurd displacement, a blending in which the good sense of lovers of birds in cages turns to mental deficiency. These displacements may "concern the confusion of the whole and of its parts (for example, the tree and the leaf or else the container and the contained,) as for instance, the slipper and the foot, the bird and the foliage, the bird and the sky, the bird and the egg." (4). Magritte identifies what reason distinguishes by virtue of successive stages which it packs away and classifies. All that is worth while and the misused principle of identity (one would say overworked) undergoes a sort of ironical erosion.

III. The aberrant superimposition. The men scattered about in the sky belong to a different order and have, so to speak, broken into the picture. They are superimposed on the sky carrying to it the logic of their upright position. For Magritte's man does not fly, does not appear to swim (which would be in a sense too normal). He is the very hallmark of an offended reality. Thus the apple on the man's face, the body on the woman's, and even the egg in place of the birds. Botticelli's *Spring* is hung like an April Fool's joke behind the little shopkeepers. But the complete coincidence of landscape and canvas in *la Condition humaine* or in *la Belle Captive* is aberrant in its very perfection: the principle of identity is ridiculed, its pretension unmasked. An old man, seated (imago of the father?) holds in one hand the fragile ostensory of pearls which reflect the shining eyes of the woman (image of the mother?). The other hand leans on a cane (or in the variants of the *Thérapeute* (1938) and of the *Domaine enchanté,* holds a wallet). But beneath the veil that falls from his hat (we see neither a head nor a body), is a white page on which are written Magritte's hieroglyphics, the key, the glass, the dove and the pipe (variants in *Thérapeute*, a sky with light clouds; in the *Domaine enchanté,* a bird in a cage). Superimposition is a sort of writing on the background of the picture. Sometimes it may consist of a beautifully written word. One might think that Magritte sabotages his own work by these painstaking graffitti. With him it is not so much the painting that is done in layers, it is the pictorial image which is stratified.

IV. Reification. We have found numerous examples of it: wherever he looks Magritte's eye immobilizes objects. What coldness there is in his blue sky, in his distant horizons, heightens the paralysis of his human beings. The little shopkeeper is a mannequin. The naked beauty in *Fleurs du Mal* (1946) turns her empty eyes towards us. At times the human figure is reduced to a jagged plank. A number of mutilations are accompanied by partial involution: that head is a box, this one an enormous glass eye, on that other the word "mountain" is written. The tree-trunk opens like a wardrobe on the secret of a cleft sphere or a lighted candle. Was not that nine-pin a woman? What living voice is degrading itself by becoming a bell tinkling as if obsessed? As for poetry, it is a pipe.

It is not ugliness that attracts Magritte: it is the emptiness of matter itself.

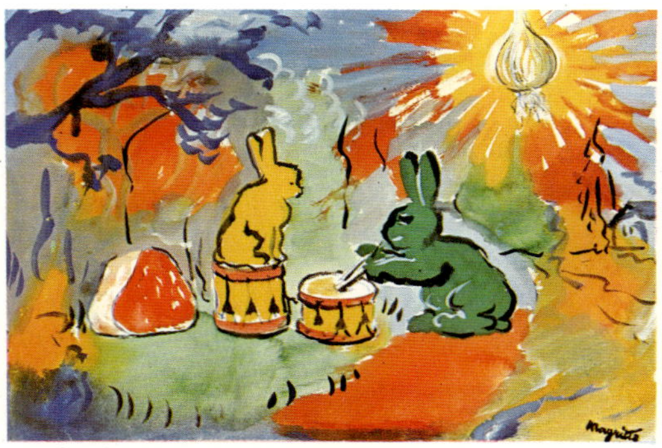

Pom Po Pom Popon Po Pompon
Gouache 1948 / 12.6 × 17.7

Not only the stonyness of the stone, but the stonyness of all things.

V. The enigmatic absolute. In Magritte's most oneiric paintings, such as *l'Assassin menacé* or *les Rêveries du promeneur solitaire*, we suspect him of giving full rein to his imagination with the deliberate intent of painting non-sense. No doubt psychologists, like surrealists, find their material in such images: both make poetry an opportunity for knowledge. For Magritte there is nothing to know. He does not brood over an undecipherable world; he puts it down as wanting in numbers. The irony of the riddle propounded suggests riddles without key. In short, categorical in itself the riddle has no hidden content, no other meaning than the non-sense to which it leads.

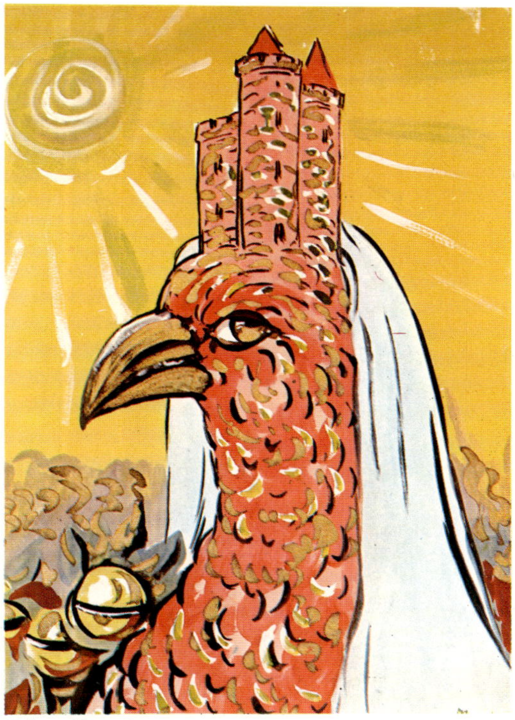

Prince Charming
Gouache 1948 / 17.7 × 12.6

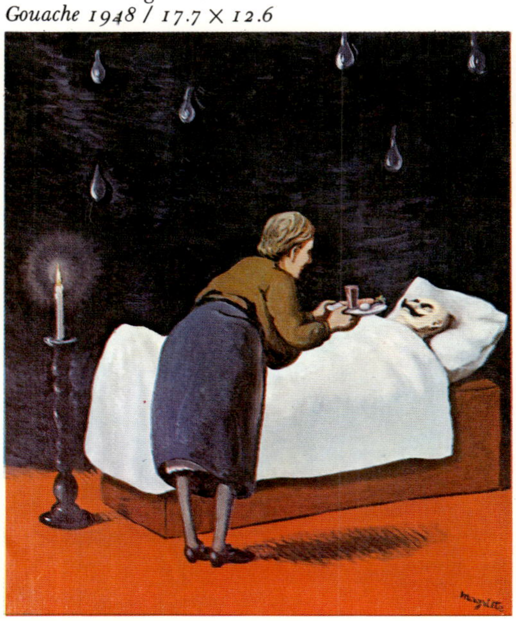

The Proof of Fire
1948 / 25.6 × 21.2

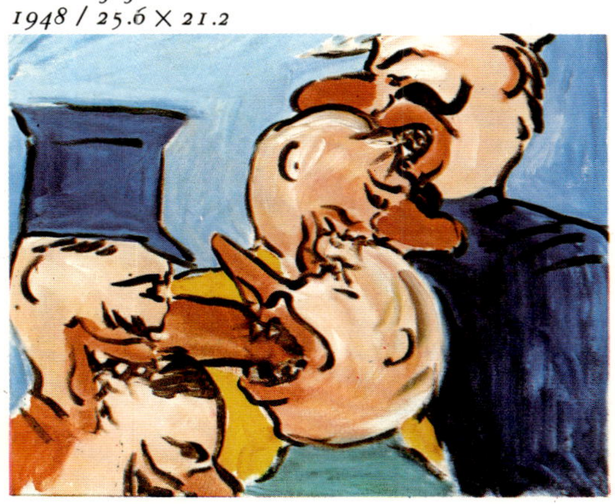

The Famine
1948 / 18.1 × 21.6

Magritte bears us out: His art, he says, "is the description of an absolute thought, that is, a thought the meaning of which remains just as unknoweable as the meaning of the world." That is why any interpretation of Magritte's works is suspect as revealing the musings of the interpreter rather the inmost themes of the interpreted. The absurd, carried to the extreme, would be that capacity for always appearing to be beyond all possible exegesis. Like the world, yes. Like Magritte.

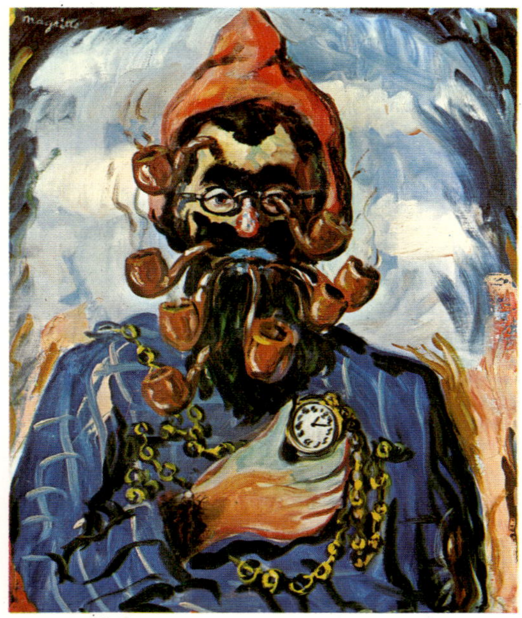

The Disabled
1948 / 23.6 × 19.6

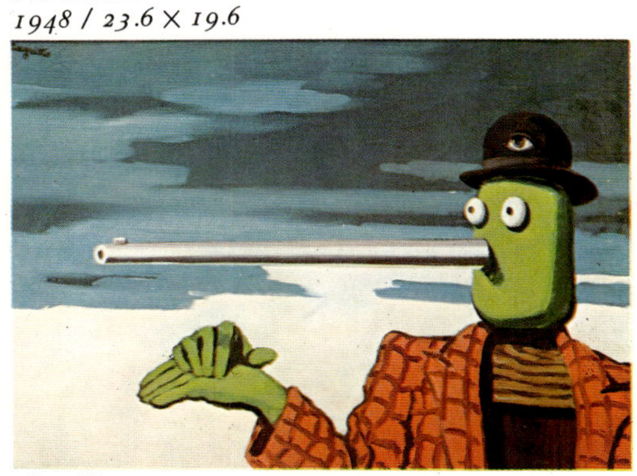

The Ellipse
1948 / 23.6 × 28.3

(1) *Qu'est-ce que la métaphysique?* (Trans. by H. Corbin) "Question I," Paris, Gallimard, 1968, pp. 41, 44 (reference to Leibnitz).

(2) Which picks up the them of *l'Éloge de la Dialectique*, 1937.

(3) Cf. *la Carte d'après Nature*, No I, Oct. 1955.

(4) José Vovelle, *le Surréalisme en Belgique*, thesis of the third cycle, unpublished. 2 vols. 1968. Vol. I, p. 259.

(5) *L'Art de la ressemblance*, Catalogue of the Magritte exhibition. Obelisk Gallery, London, 1963.

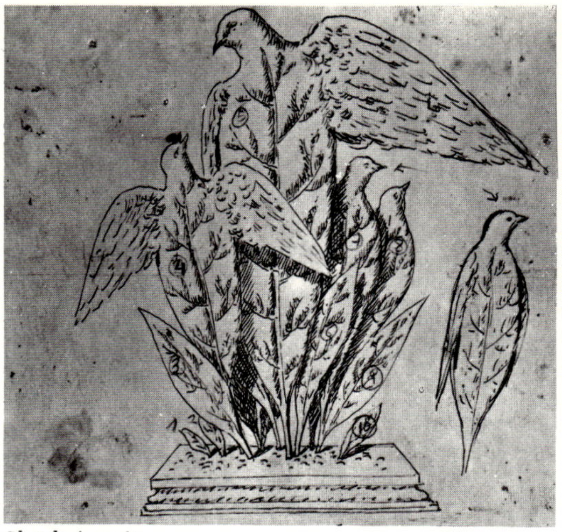
Sketch / 1967

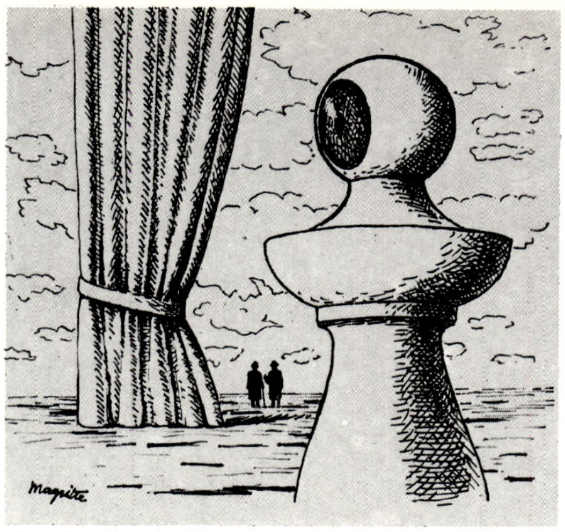
Drawing / 1960 (?)

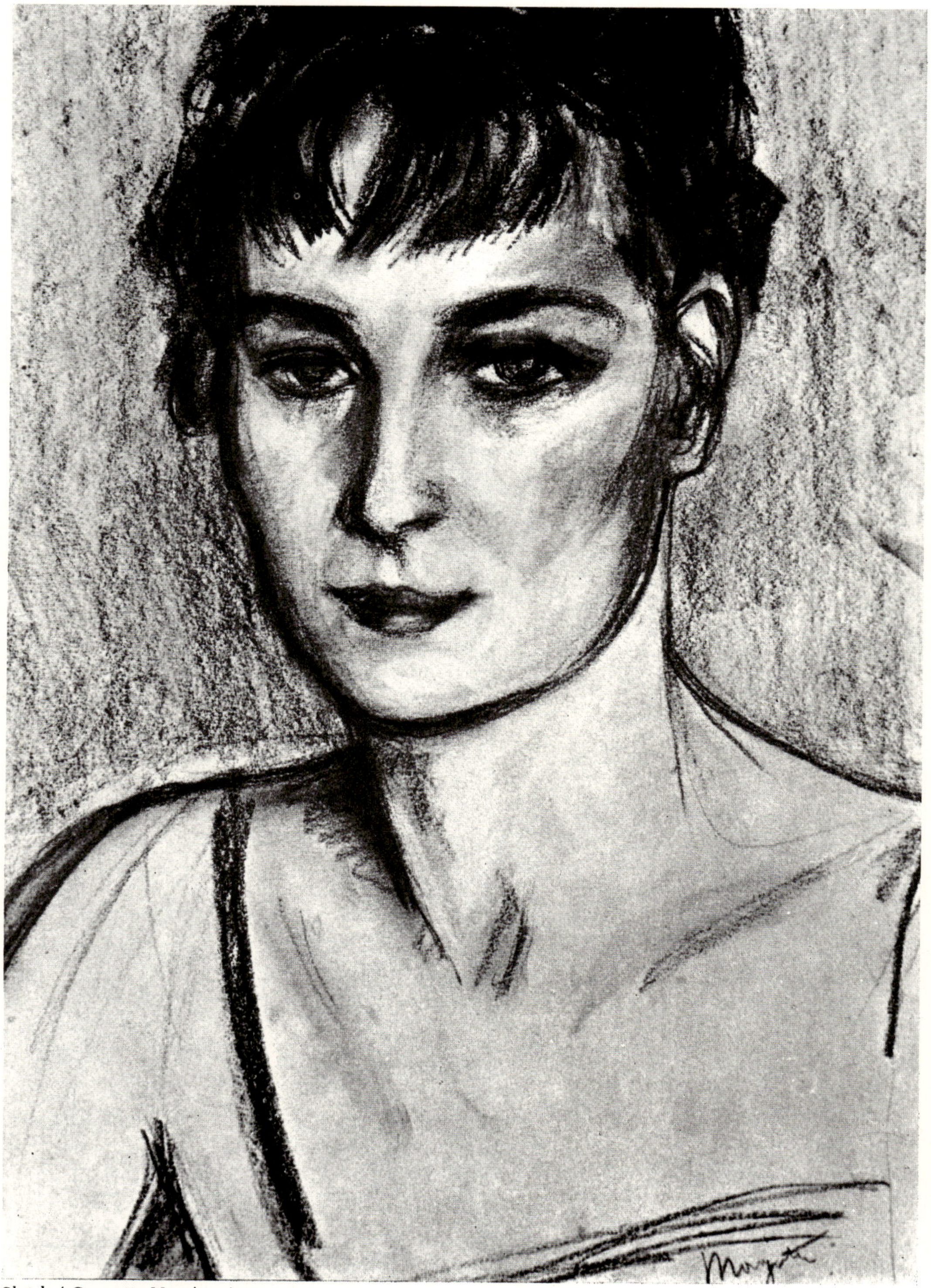
Sketch / Georgette Magritte / 1924

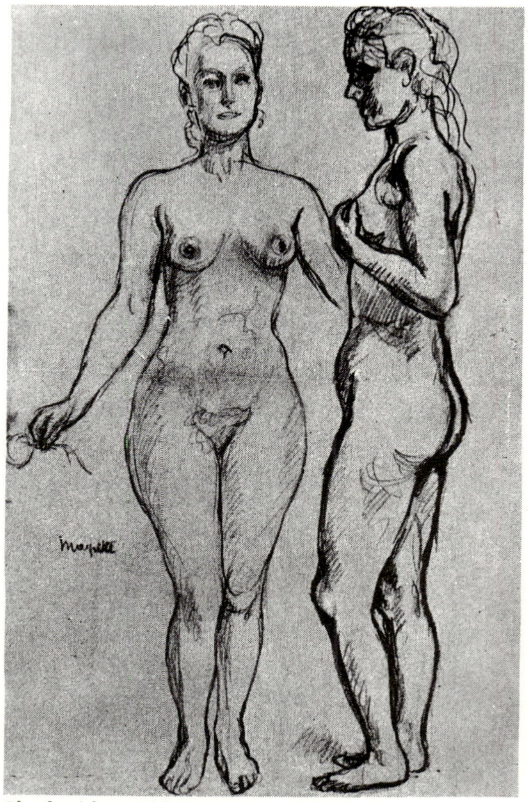
Sketch without Title / 1936

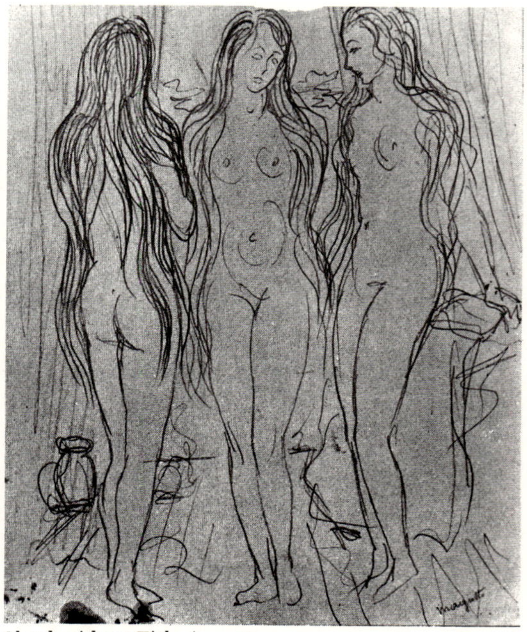
Sketch without Title / 1936

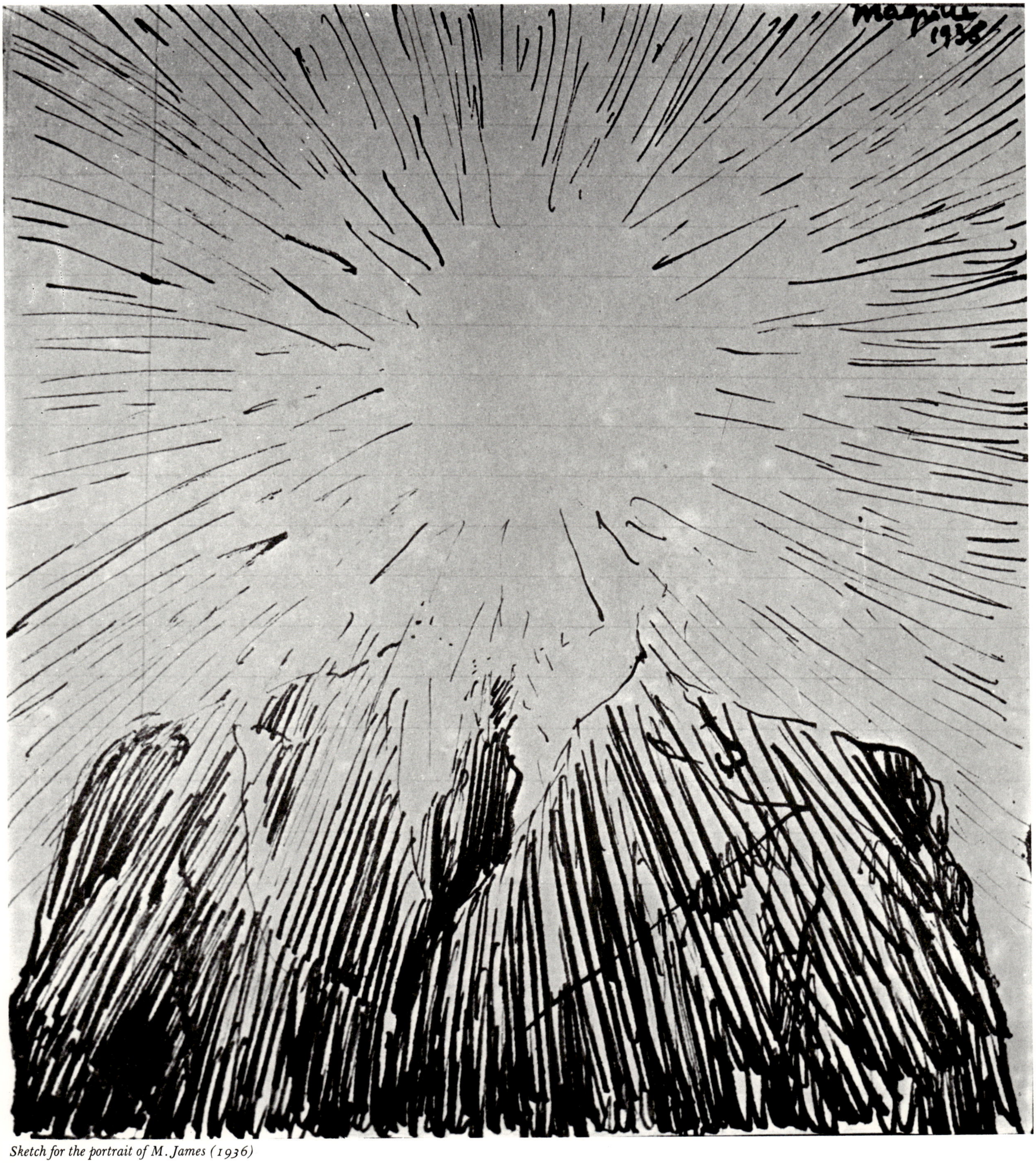

Sketch for the portrait of M. James (1936)

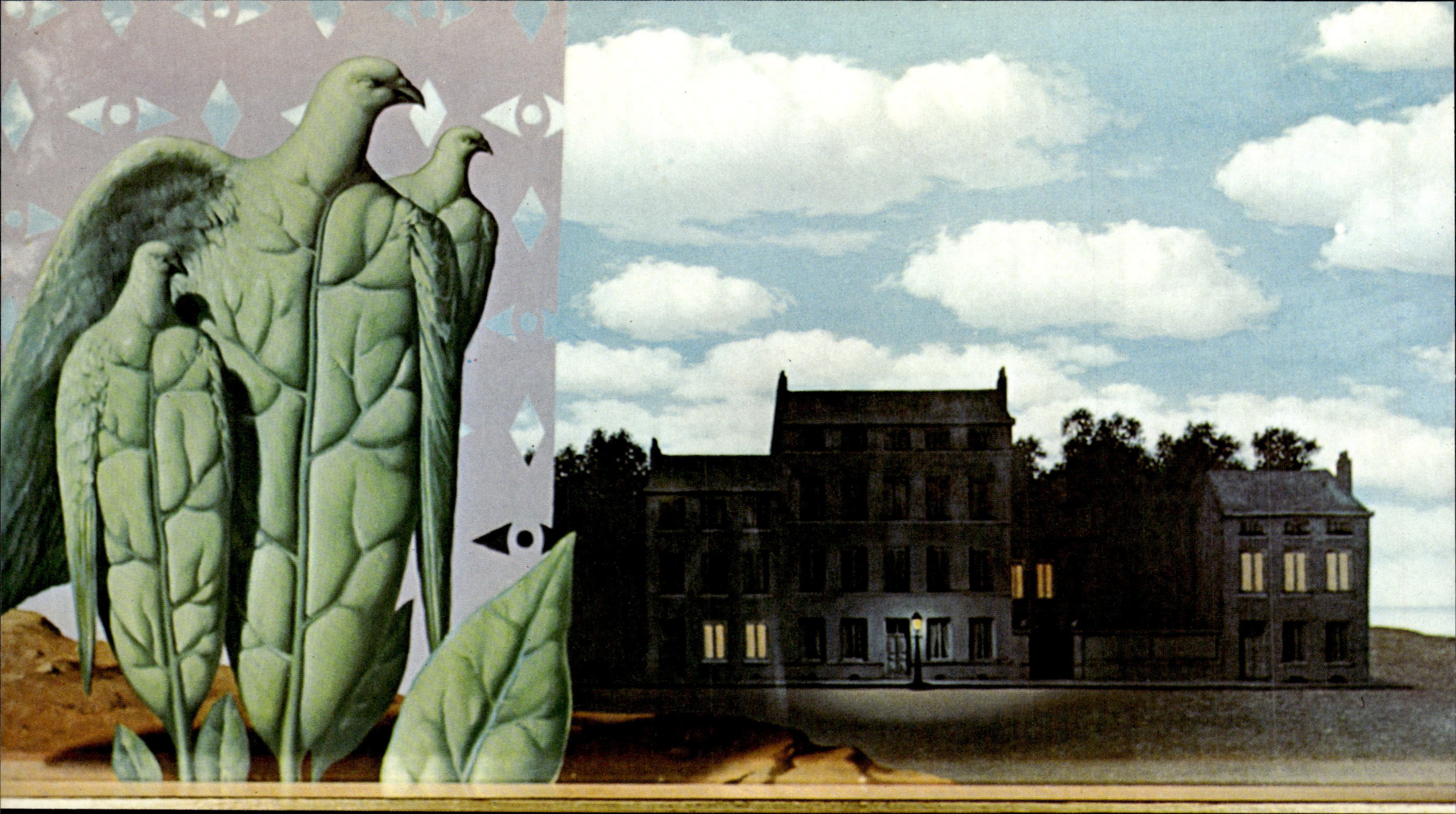

The Enchanted Domain. Salle du Lustre of the Casino of Knokke. About 72 yards circumference. 1952.

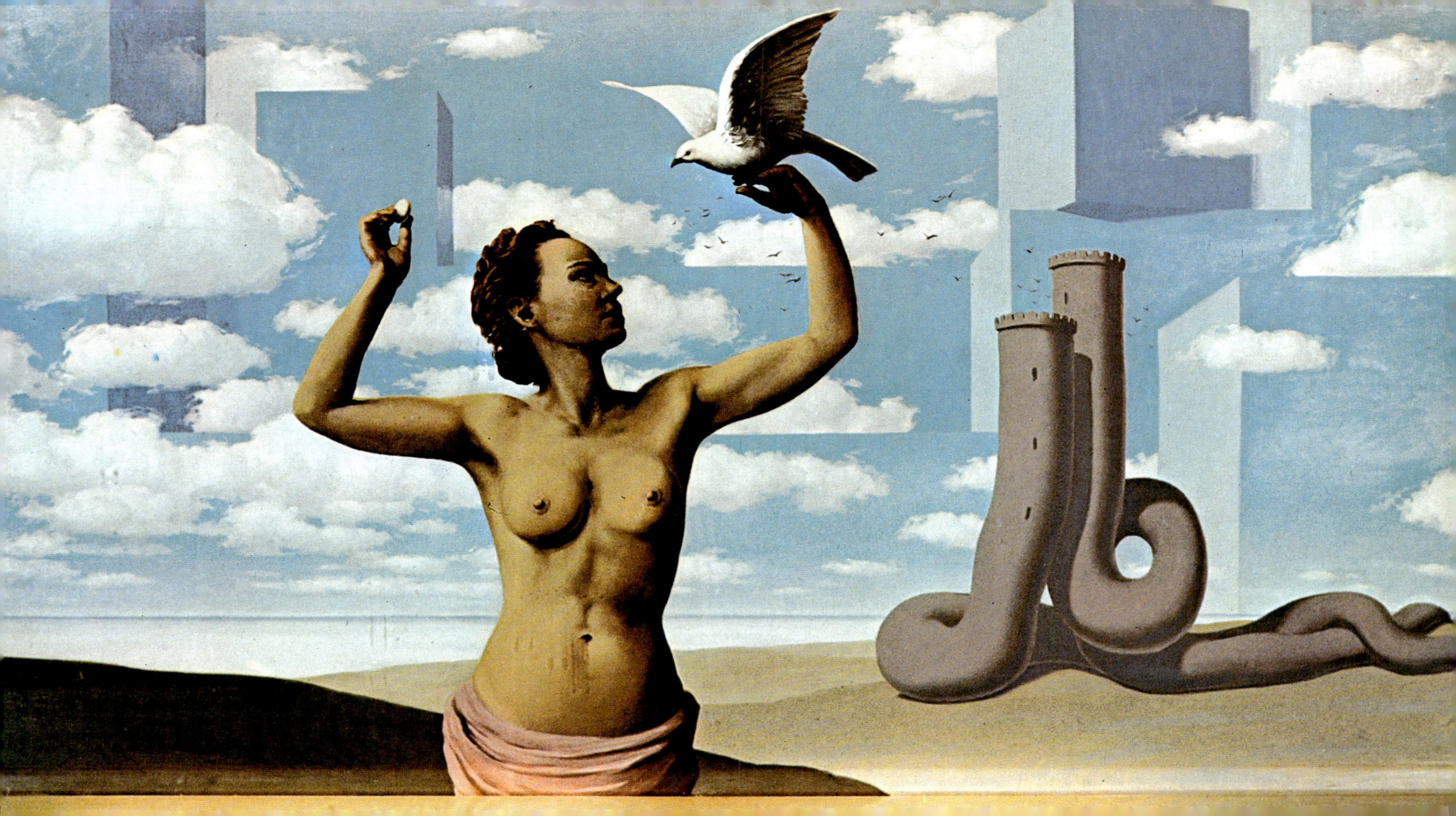

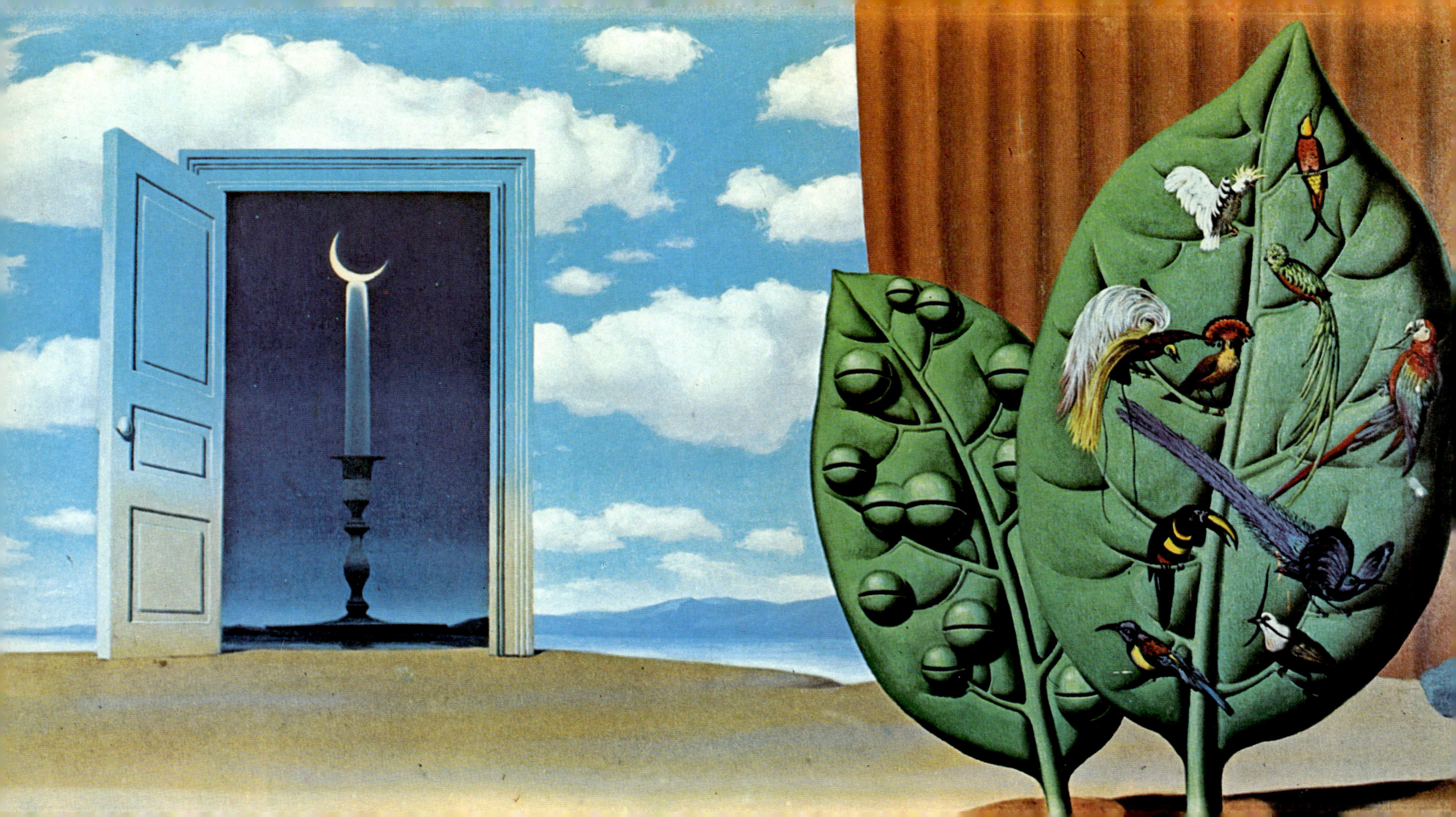

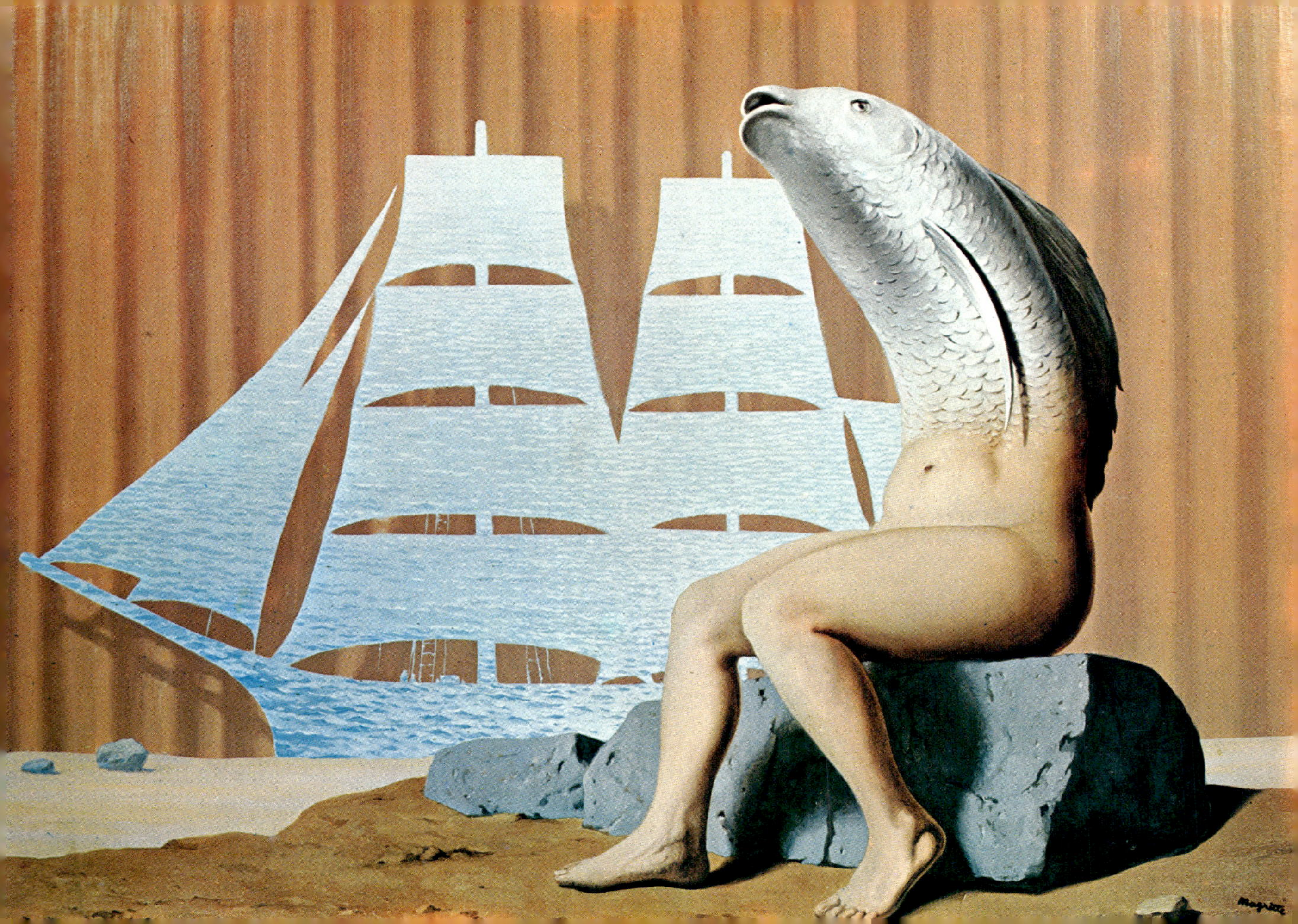

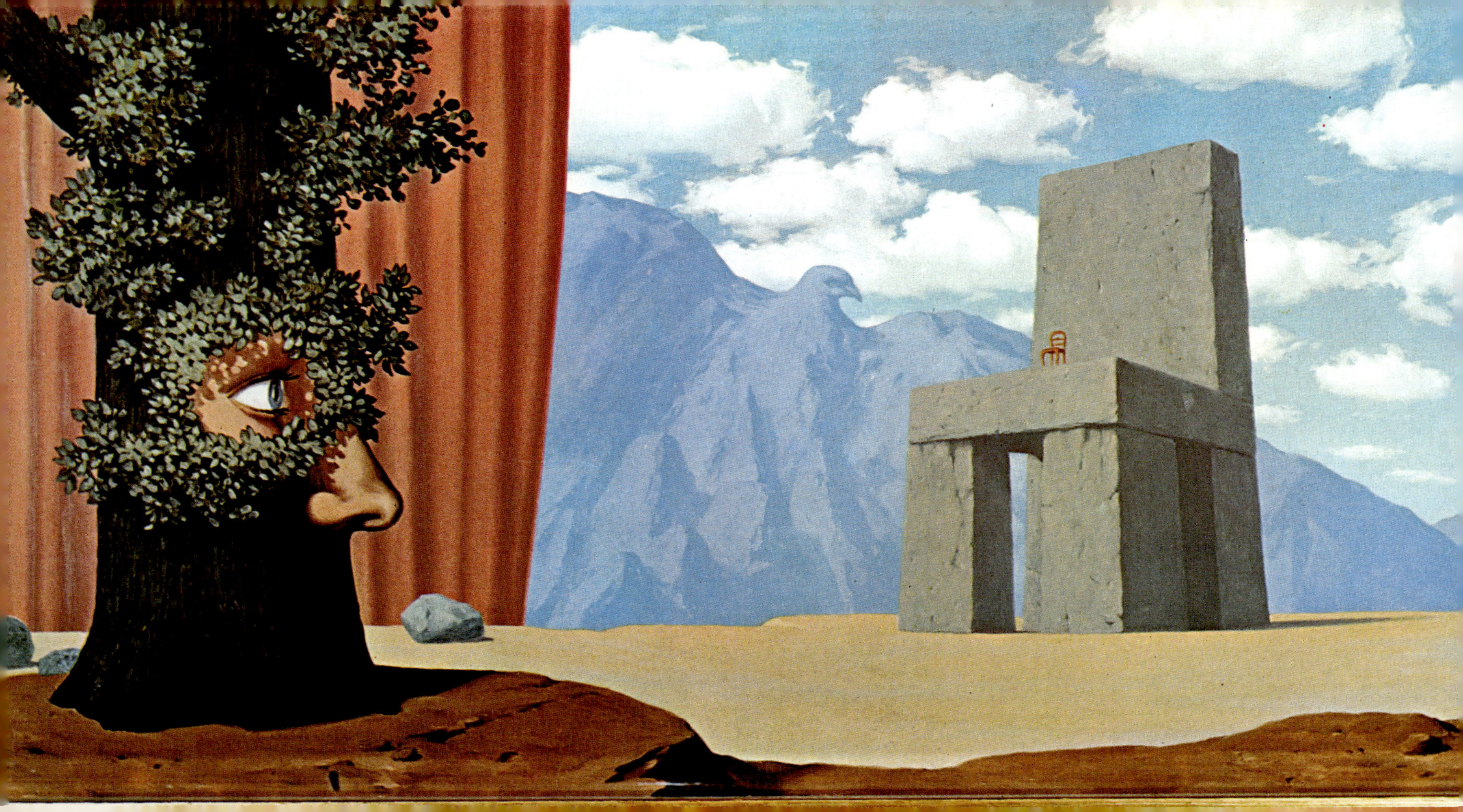

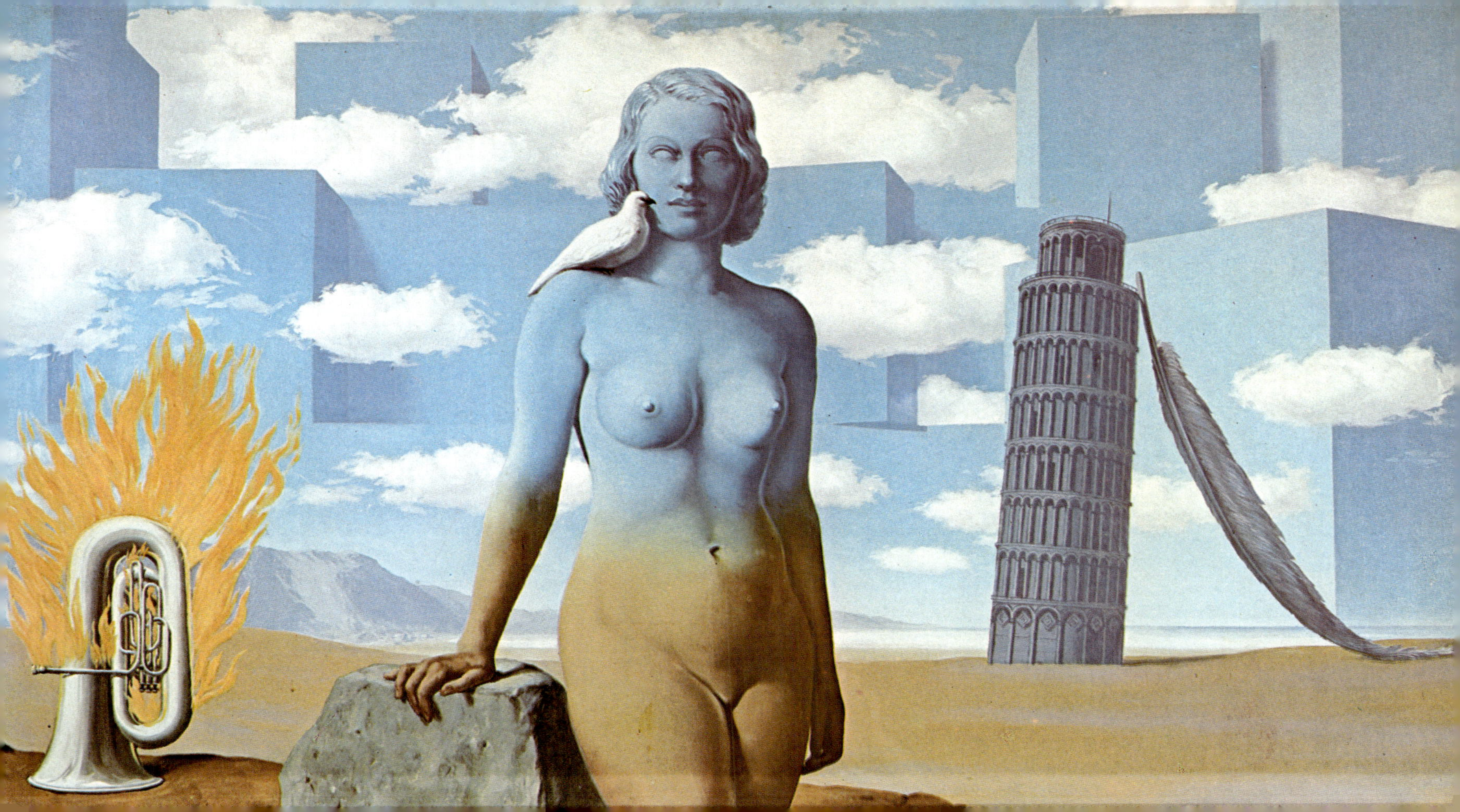

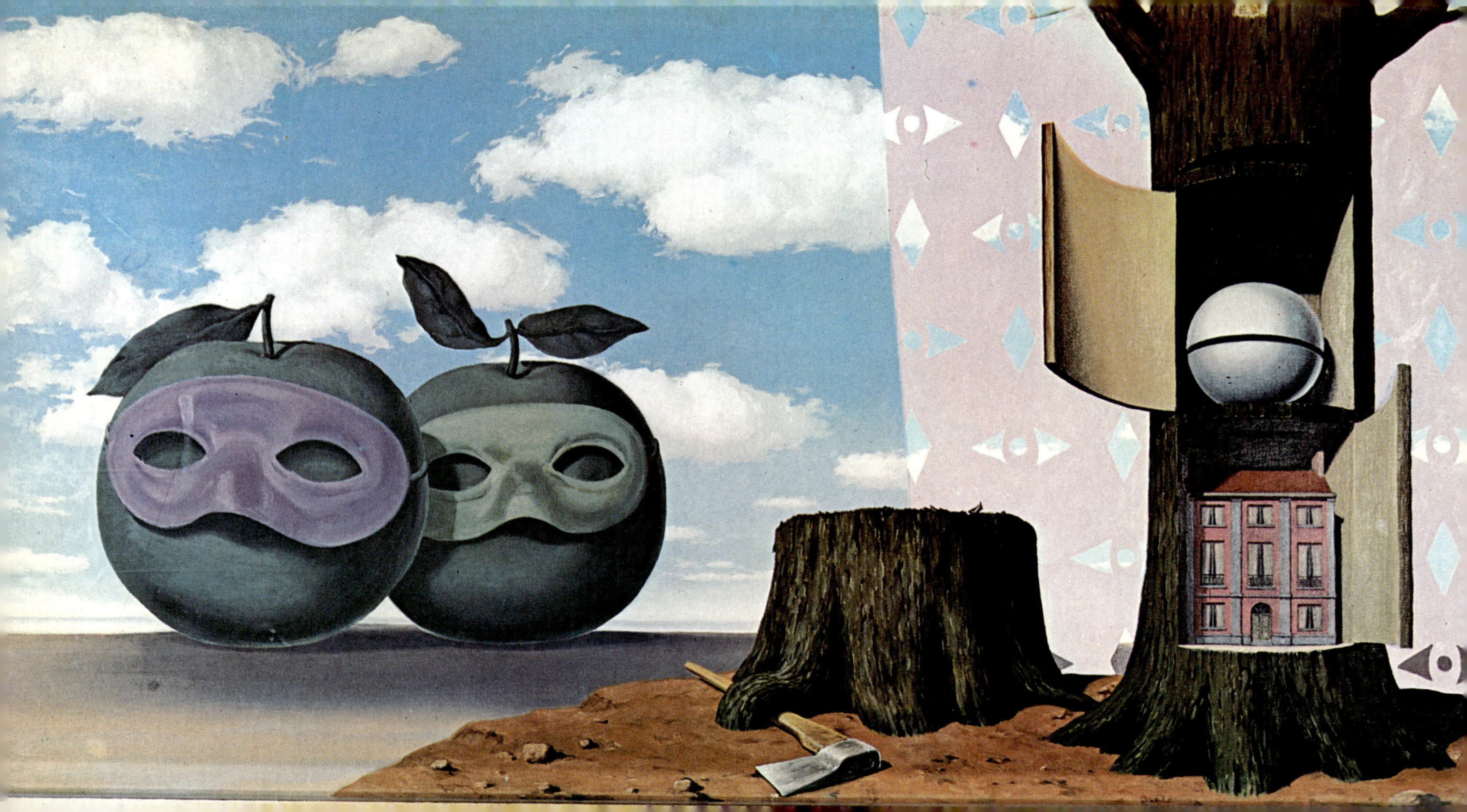

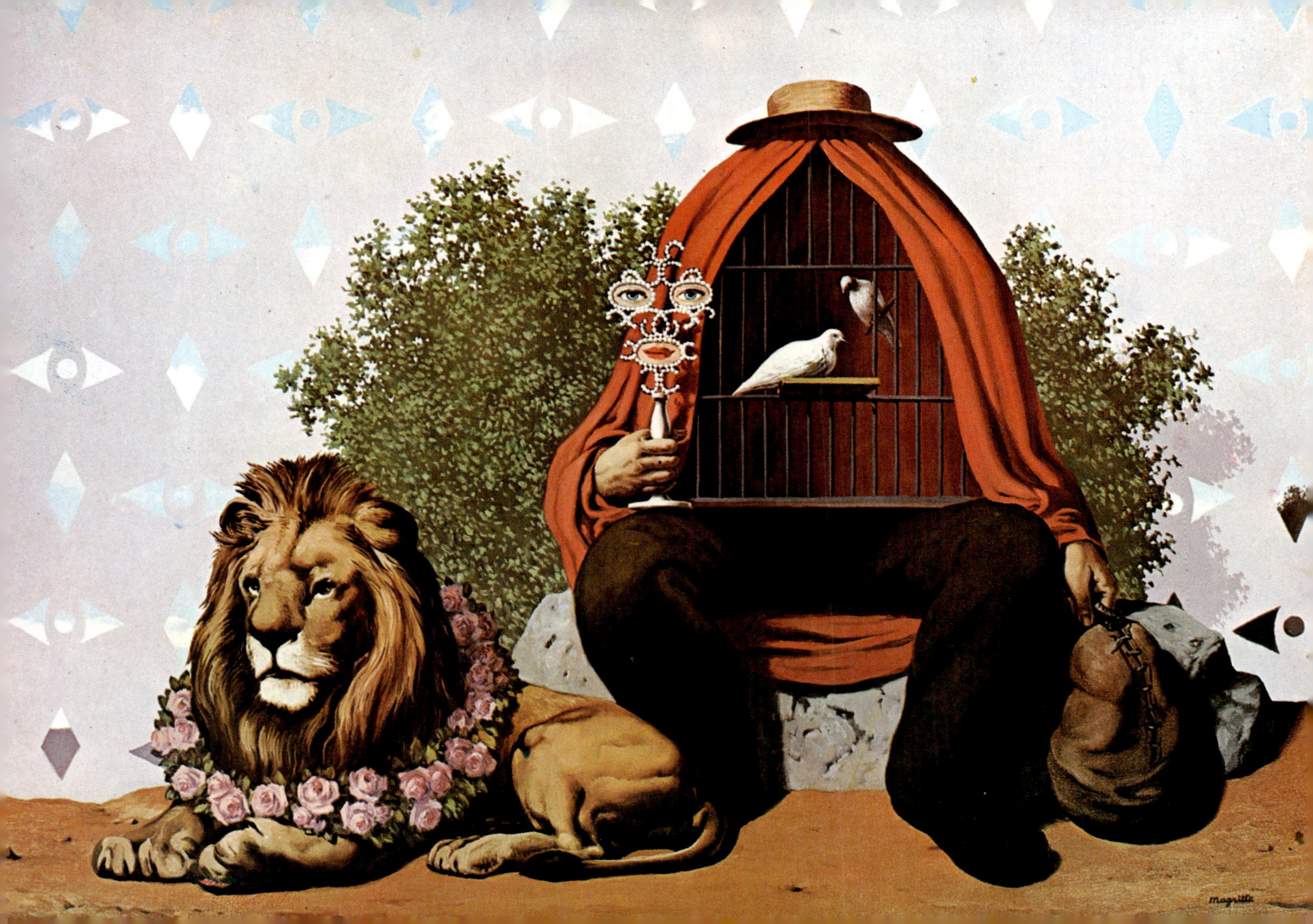
Magritte

BIOGRAPHY OF RENE MAGRITTE

1898 November 21, born at Lessines (Hainaut). His father is a wholesale merchant. The family, which had three sons, René, Raymond and Paul, was to move several times. In Gilly, story of the captive balloon that fell on their house.
1904 or 1905 Story of the painter met in the cemetery where René was playing with a little girl.
1912 At Châtelet one night René's mother, Régina, throws herself into the Sambre. René devoted to Paul. Shocks his father's servants by pretending and mimicking excessive piety.
1913 At Charleroi, on a merry-go-round at the fair, he meets Georgette Berger, thirteen years old. The two children constantly together, but finally separate. René infatuated by the films of *Fantomas*.
1915 First impressionistic paintings.
1916 Leaves school and goes to Brussels to enter the Académie des Beaux-Arts. Not very diligent pupil.
1918 Discusses cubism and...
1919 ... discovers futurism.
1920 Meets Georgette Berger again by chance. Exhibits for the first time in Brussels. Meets the future Belgian surrealists: Mesens, Nougé, Goemans. Lecomte show him a reproduction of de Chirico: crucial shock.
1921 Military service.
1922 Marries Georgette Berger. Works in the Peter Lacroix wallpaper factory at Haren.
1922-1923 "Abstract" period, with Servranck.
1925 First surrealist work: *le Jockey perdu*. He sometimes paints a picture a day.
1926-1927 First period: disturbing and somber scenes.
1926 *L'Ange migrateur, les Rêveries du Promeneur solitaire, la Naissance de l'Idole*. Publishes "Marie," bi-monthly magazine for young people. In Paris, meets surrealists, makes friends with Breton and Eluard. Backed by Le Centaure gallery in Brussels, he devotes himself solely to painting.
1927 *L'Oasis, l'Assassin menacé*. First one-man exhibition, at Le Centaure. Little response from the public. Settles at Perreux-sur-Marne.
1927-1940 Second period: cold and clear tones.
1928 *Le Temps menaçant*.
1929 First quarrel with André Breton.
1930 Returns to Brussels. Exhibits collages with the surrealists at Goemans'.
1934 *Le Mouvement perpétuel, la Condition humaine, le Viol*.
1936 *Le Modèle rouge*. First exhibition in the United States, Julien Levy gallery, New York.
1938 Exhibits at the London gallery.
1939 Stays in Belgium for the duration of the war.
1940-1946 Period of "full sunlight." Technique close to Renoir.
1941-1948 Exhibits regularly at Dietrich gallery, Brussels.
1943 *Le Vertige*.
1945 Joins the Belgian Communist Party. Swift disillusionment.
1946 "Alice in Wonderland." Joins the "revolutionary surrealists." Another quarrel with Breton.
1947 *Le Carnaval du Sage, la Philosophie dans le Boudoir*.
1947 For three months, "vache" period.
1948 Exhibition in New York and in Hollywood. Showed twenty canvasses and gouaches (period "vache"), Galerie du Faubourg, Paris. Then *le Chant d'Amour, la Mémoire, la Liberté de l'Esprit*.
1950 *Les Travaux d'Alexandre*.
1950-1955 *Thèmes du cercueil et trompe-l'œil de glaise*.
1951 *Perspectives, Madame Récamier*, after David, *l'Explication*.
1952 Published the review *la Carte d'après Nature* (1952-1955).
1953 *Le Domaine enchanté*, mural painting, Casino of Knokke-le-Zoute. Exhibits in New York at Iolas; in London, the Lefèvre Gallery; in Rome, Obelisco Gallery; in Paris, l'Étoile scellée.
1954 First large Magritte retrospective, Palais des Beaux-Arts, Brussels. Variant of *l'Empire des Lumières*.
1956 Guggenheim Prize for Belgium.
1957 *La fée ignorante*, mural painting in the Palais des Beaux-Arts in Charleroi. Exhibited at Iolas in New York in 1957, 1958 and 1959.

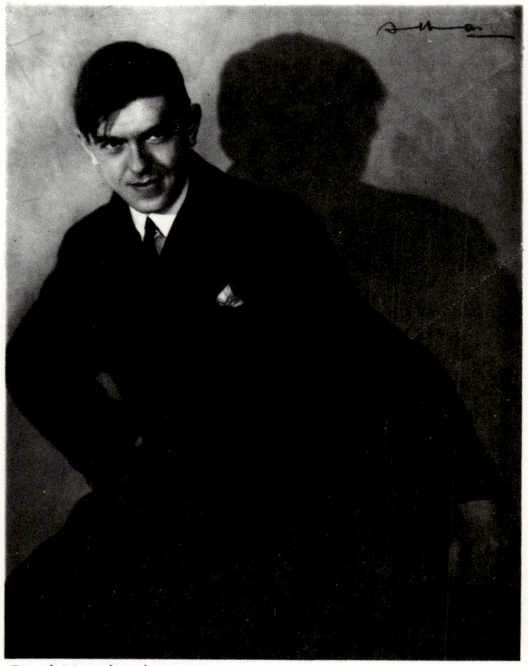

René Magritte in 1924

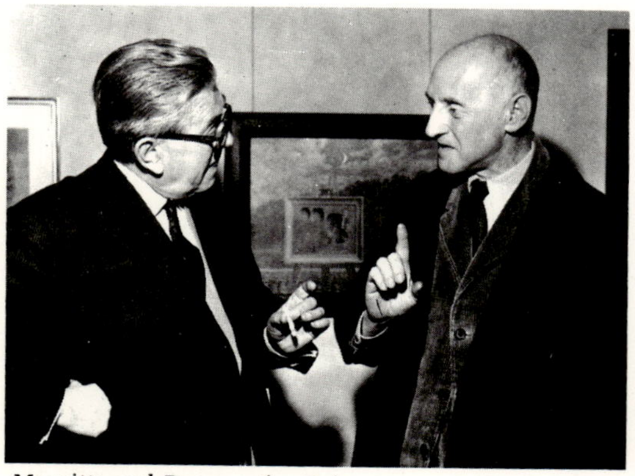

Magritte and Brauner (1960)

1960 Works for the review *Rhétorique* (1961-1964). Exhibits in Dallas and in Houston. Paints *la Folie des Grandeurs*.
1962 Magritte's works, Casino of Knokke-le-Zoute. Exhibits at Schwartz in Milan; at Iolas in New-York; and at the Walker Art Center in Minneapolis. Says: "Breton has always been a friend."
1964 Exposition Magritte, *le Sens propre*, Iolas Gallery, Paris. Foreword by Breton.
1965-1966 Magritte Retrospective at the Museum of Modern Art, New York. Certain of his paintings taken up in bronze sculptures which are to be exhibited at Iolas in Paris in 1968.
1967 Death of René Magritte, August 15, in Brussels.

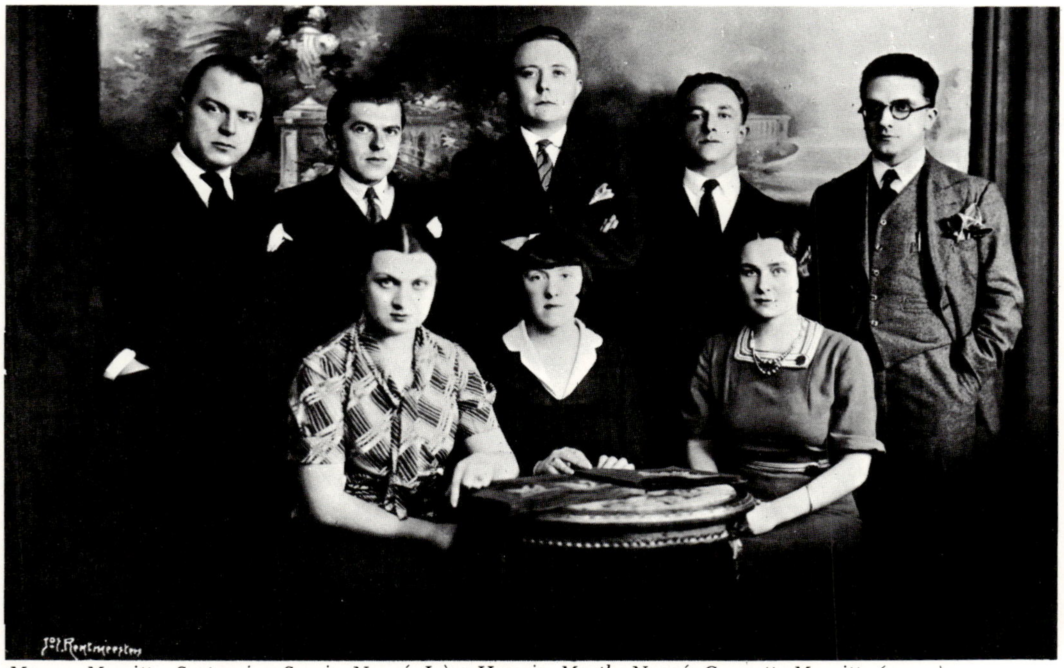

Mesens, Magritte, Scutenaire, Souris, Nougé, Irène Hamoir, Marthe Nougé, Georgette Magritte (1934)

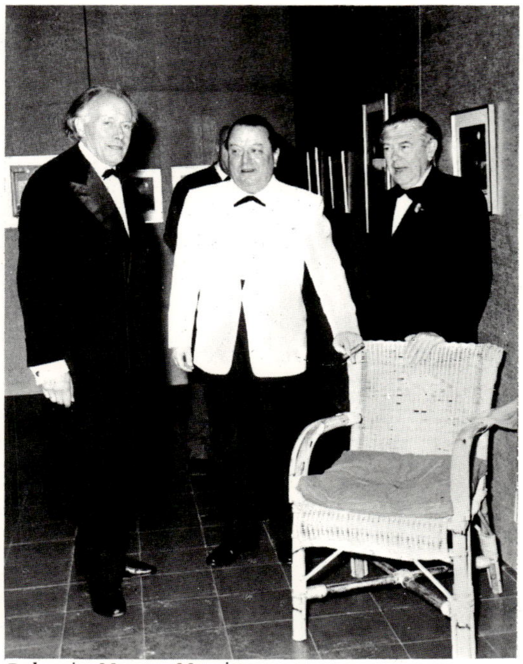

Delvaux, Mesens, Magritte

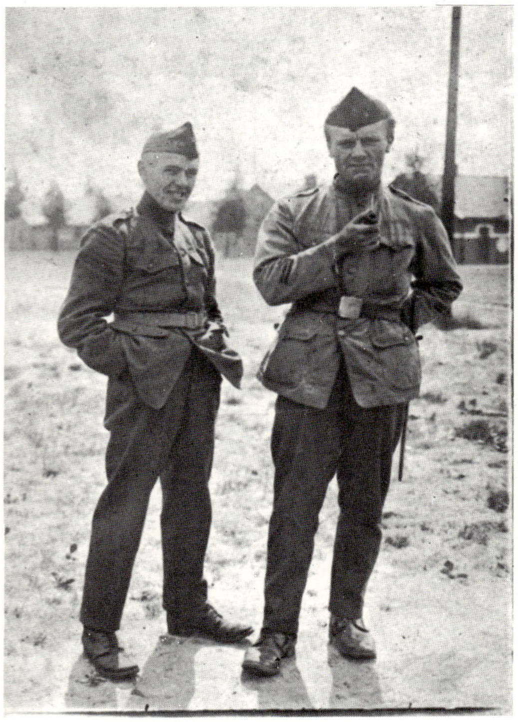

Magritte and Pierre Bourgeois (1921)

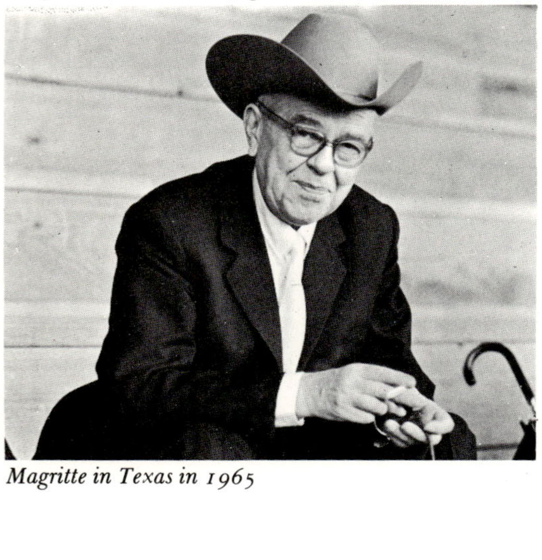

Magritte in Texas in 1965

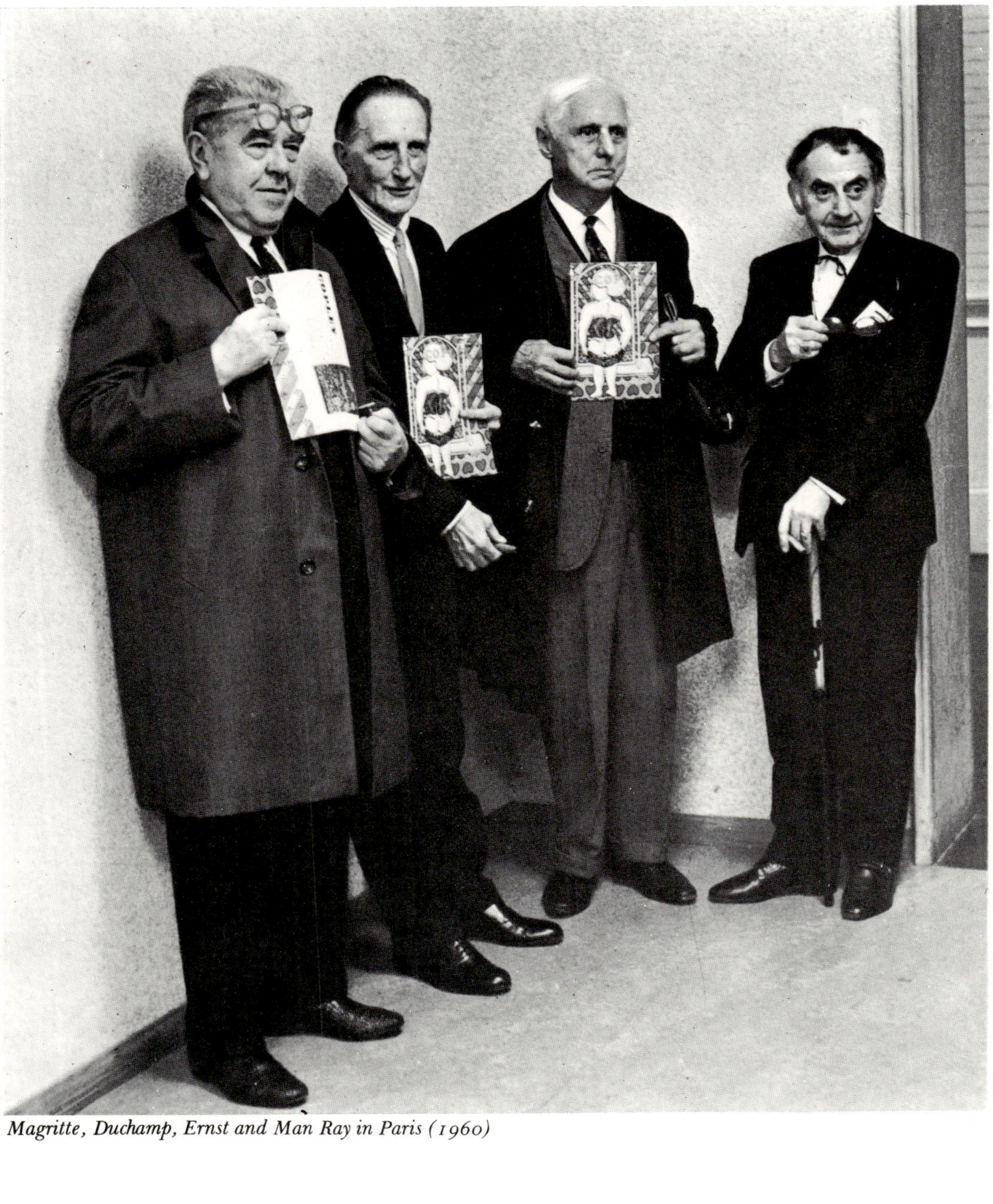

Magritte, Duchamp, Ernst and Man Ray in Paris (1960)

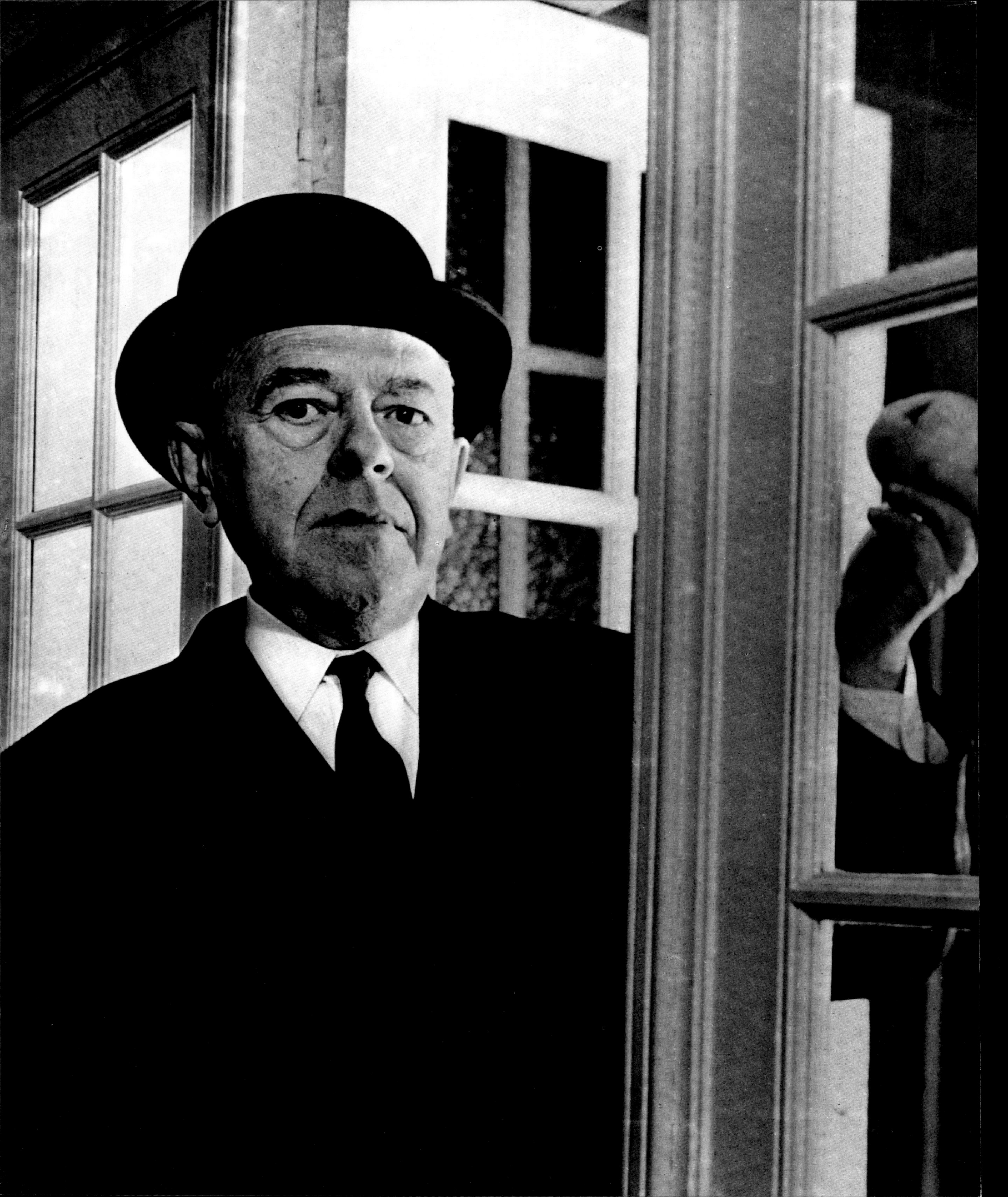

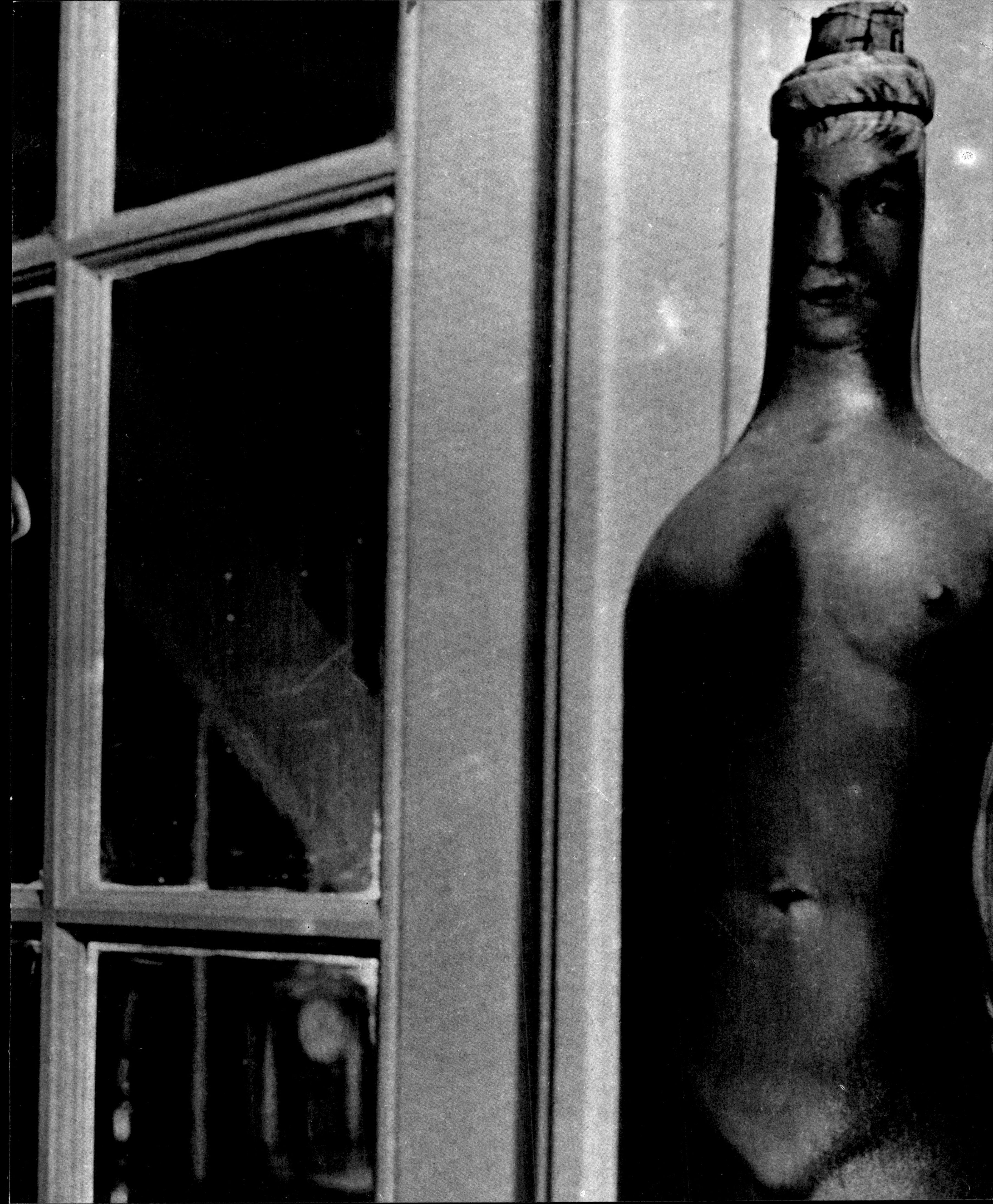

SELECTED BIBLIOGRAPHY

monographs and books

Demarne, Pierre. René Magritte. Tilleur-lez-Liège, André Bosmans, 1961.

Gablik, Suzi. Magritte, Greenwich, Connecticut, New York Graphic Society, 1970.

Gomez-Correa, Enrique. El espetro de René Magritte. Santiago de Chile, Ediciones Mandrágora, 1948.

Marcien, Marcel. Magritte. Brussels, les Auteurs associés, 1943.

Nougé, Paul. René Magritte ou les images défendues. Brussels, les Auteurs associés, 1943.

Scutenaire, Louis. Brussels, Éditions Librairie Sélection, 1947.

Scutenaire, Louis. René Magritte. Brussels, ministère de l'Éducation nationale et de la Culture, 1964.

Scutenaire, Louis. Magritte. Chicago, Will and Nora Copley Foundation, 1958.

Soby, James Thrall. René Magritte, New York, The Museum of Modern Art, 1965.

Waldberg, Patrick. René Magritte. Brussels, De Rache, 1965.

articles

Amphoux, Georges d'. Conversation avec un surréaliste. Les idées de René Magritte. Cahiers d'art. Feb. 1, 1958, p. 712-714.

Foucault, Michel. "Ceci n'est pas une pipe." "Cahiers du Chemin," Paris, Gallimard, January 1968, p. 77-105.

Goemans, Camille. La jeune peinture belge. Bulletin de la vie artistique, Paris, Sept. 1, 1926, p. 266-269.

Jaguer, Édouard. Au pays des images défendues. "Aujourd'hui," June 1960, p. 10-19.

Jaguer, Édouard. Quelques images du Nord. Front unique. Milan. Nouvelle série No. 2. Autumn, 1960, p. 10-17.

Jaguer, Édouard. Accent circonspect. Phases No. 9. April 1964, p. 11-19, 64-66.

Jouffroy, Alain. Le rayon invisible du surréalisme. Jardin des arts. January 1960, p. 30-39.

Langui, Émile. René Magritte. Belgich Schilder. Kroniek van hedendaagsche Kunst en Kultur. Amsterdam. August 15, 1939, p. 313-315.

Lecomte, Marcel. Quelques tableaux de Magritte et les textes qu'ils ont suscités. Bulletin des Musées royaux, No. 1-2, 1964, p. 101-110.

Mesens, E.L.T. The cabinet of curiosities. The world of René Magritte. The Saturday Book, No. 19, p. 273-276.

Michaux, Henri. En rêvant à partir de peintures énigmatiques. Mercure de France. December 1964, p. 585-599.

Scutenaire, Louis. En parlant un peu de Magritte. Cahiers d'art, Vol. XXX (1955), p. 254-264.

Stevo, Jean. Le surréalisme et la peinture en Belgique. L'art belge. Numéro spécial René Magritte. January 1968, p. 55-62.

Tatigushi, Shuzo. René Magritte. Mizue. June 1939, p. 644-649.

Van Hecke, Pierre-Gustave. René Magritte, peintre de la pensée abstraite. Sélection. March 1927, p. 439-444.

Waldberg, Patrick. René Magritte, l'inspiration et le mystère. XXe siècle, new series, No. 22. December 1963, p. 10-18.

To complete this bibliography, the reader is advised to consult the general bibliography (1919-1965) by André Blavier which can be found in René Magritte by Patrick Waldberg, cited above.

general works

Alexandrian, Sarane. Surrealist Art, London, Thames and Hudson, and New York, Praeger, 1970.

Breton André. Le surréalisme et la peinture. 3rd edition. Paris. Gallimard, 1965.

Gascoyne, David. A Short Survey of Surrealism. London. Cobden-Sanderson, 1935.

Jean, Marcel and Mezei, Arpad. A History of Surrealist Painting. London, Weidenfeld and Nicolson, and New York, Grove Press, 1960.

Levy, Julien. Surrealism. New York. The Black Sun Press, 1936.

Nadeau, Maurice. The History of Surrealism. New York. Macmillan, 1965.

Passeron, René. Histoire de la peinture surréaliste. Paris. Le livre de poche illustré, 1968.

Raynal, Maurice, Modern Painting. Geneva. Skira, 1953.

Rubin, William S. Dada, Surrealism and Their Heritage. New York. The Museum of Modern Art, 1968.

Waldberg, Patrick. Surrealism. Lausanne, Skira, 1962.

Waldberg, Patrick. Surrealism (a Documentary Anthology). London, Thames and Hudson, and New York, McGraw-Hill, 1966.

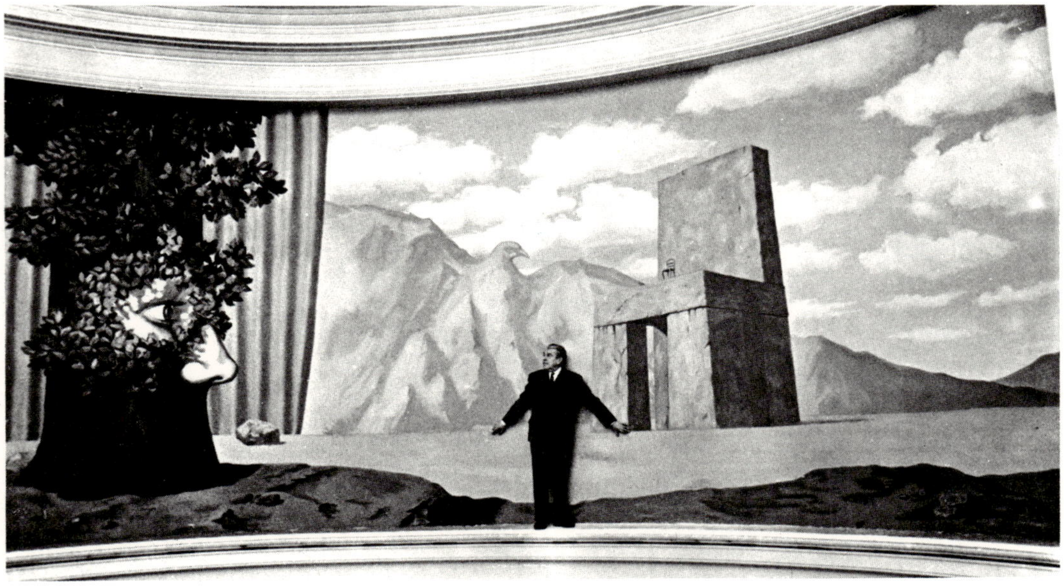

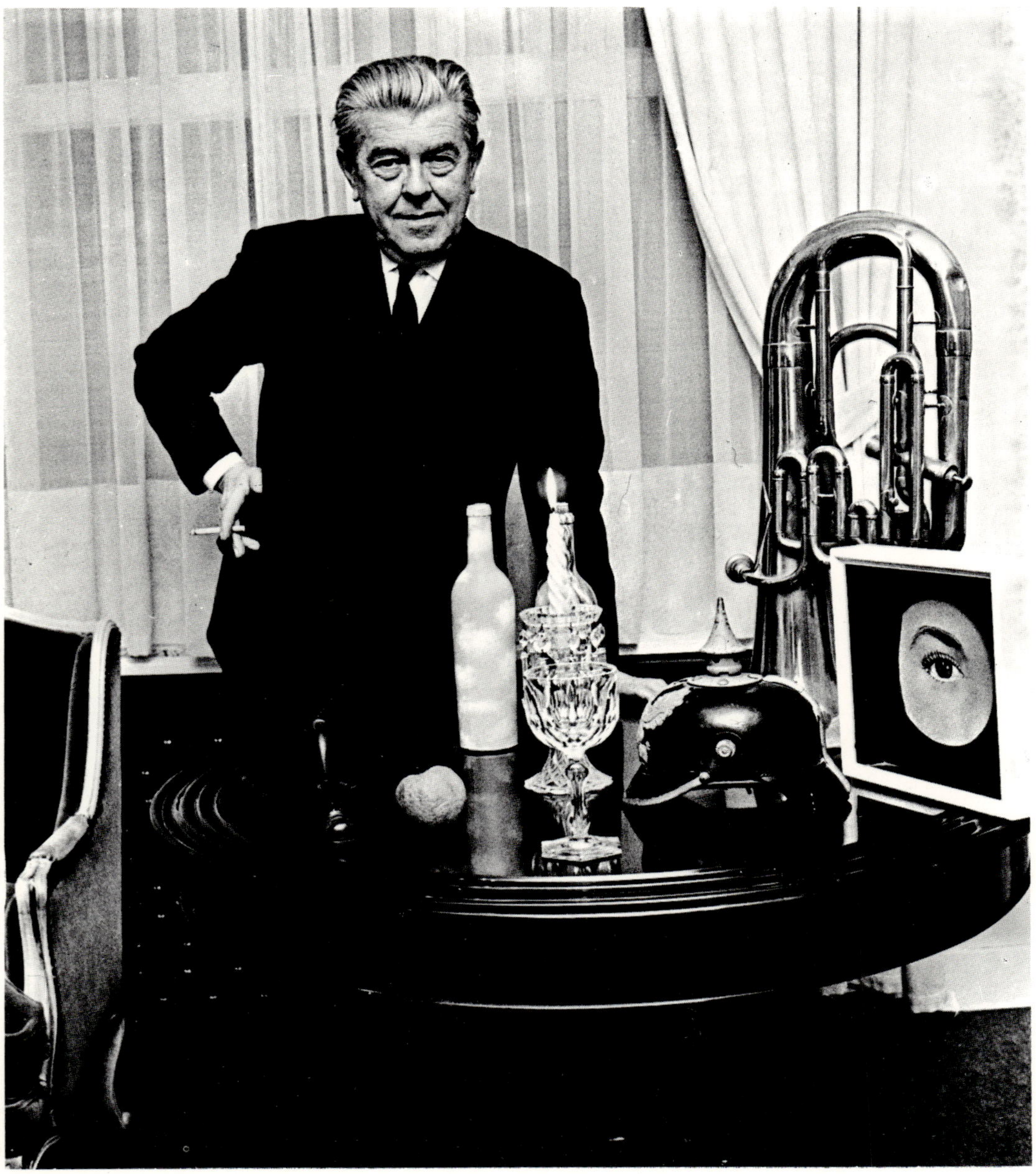

principal writings of René Magritte

Aphorismes, "391," No. 19, Oct. 1924, p. 4.

L'homme au visage sans chemin. Théâtre en plein cœur de la vie; Distances, No. 1, Paris, Feb. 1928. Other texts are in No. 1 and 2.

Les mots et les images (answer to an inquiry on love); la Révolution surréaliste, No. 12, Dec. 1929, p. 32-33.

La ligne de vie; Combat, Brussels, Dec. 10, 1938, and l'Invention collective, No. 2, April 1940.

Le surréalisme en plein soleil. L'expérience continue. Manifeste No. 1, Brussels, le Miroir infidèle, Oct. 1946 (collective).

Le soleil et le prêtre. Faits divers; le Surractuel, Brussels, No. 1, 1948.

Je pense à de nouvelles recherches; la Carte d'après Nature, Brussels, No. 1, Oct. 1952.

Les annonces du petit Gérard. Nat Pinkerton; la Carte d'après Nature, No. 4, April 1953.

Un art poétique; la Carte d'après Nature, No. 8, Jan. 1955.

Answer to the inquiry "Situation de la peinture en 1954"; Medium No. 4, Jan. 1955, p. 43-45.

Answer to the inquiry "Quelle est votre conception de l'art fantastique et magique?" Tafelronde, Anvers, Special No. V, 3-5, 1959; Fantasmagorie, p. 59.

De kunst van de gelijkenis; Kroniek van Kunst en Kultur, XXI, 8, 1961, p. 49-51.

Le rappel à l'ordre rhétorique, Tilleur-lez-Liège, No. 1, 1961.

La voix du mystère; *ibid,* No. 4, 1962.

Une fausse idée; *ibid,* No. 5, 1962.

Leçon de choses; *ibid,* No. 7, 1962.

Ma conception de l'art de peindre. Le temps passe. Déclaration. Rhétorique, No. 12, August 1964.

It is a pleasure to thank here the museums and collectors who have kindly given us their help, among them : Moore International Studio, New York; Greenwich Fine Arts, Connecticut; Liberart; Blue Moon Gallery, New York; Charles Byron, New York; Harriett Griffin, New York; Mme Berger, Brussels; Mr. William N. Copley, New York; Mrs. John de Cuevas, New York; the Belgian State; Messrs. Nesuhi and Ahmet Ertegun, New York; M. Isy Brachot, Brussels; M. Alexandre Iolas, Paris; M. Marc Hendrickx, Brussels; M. Claude Hersaint, Paris; Mme and M. Henri Jeanson, Paris; Mme Jean Krebs; M. Charles Kriwin, Brussels; The Los Angeles County Museum of Art (Gift of Mr. W.N. Copley); M. Claude Marcy; Mrs. Dominique and Mr. Jean de Menil, Houston; Mr. W.H. Nelly, London; MM. Jacques Nellens, Gustave Nellens, Knokke; Roger Nellens; Ladies Oranmore and Browne; Mme Salik, Brussels; M. Scheidweiler; M. Claude Spaak, Brussels; Mr. Harry Torcziner, New York; University of St Thomas, Houston; Mme and M. M.J.B. Urvater, Rhode-Saint-Genèse; M.P.G. Van Ecke, Brussels.

The photographs are by Jean-Pierre Lebert, Paul Bitjebier, Jean-Jacques Damour, Daniel Filipacchi and Malcolm Varon.

The measurements of all works illustrated in this volume are given in inches; height precedes width.

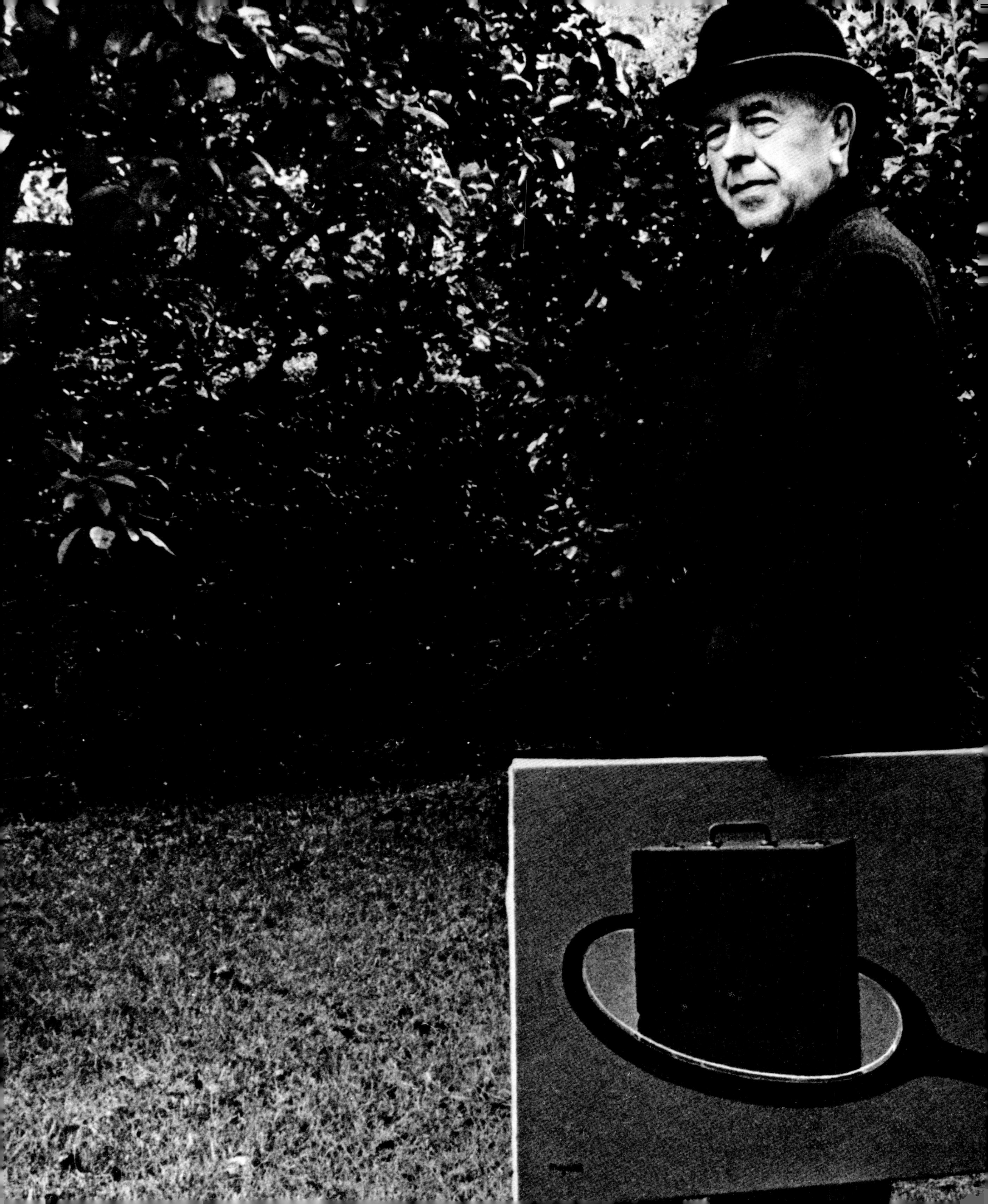

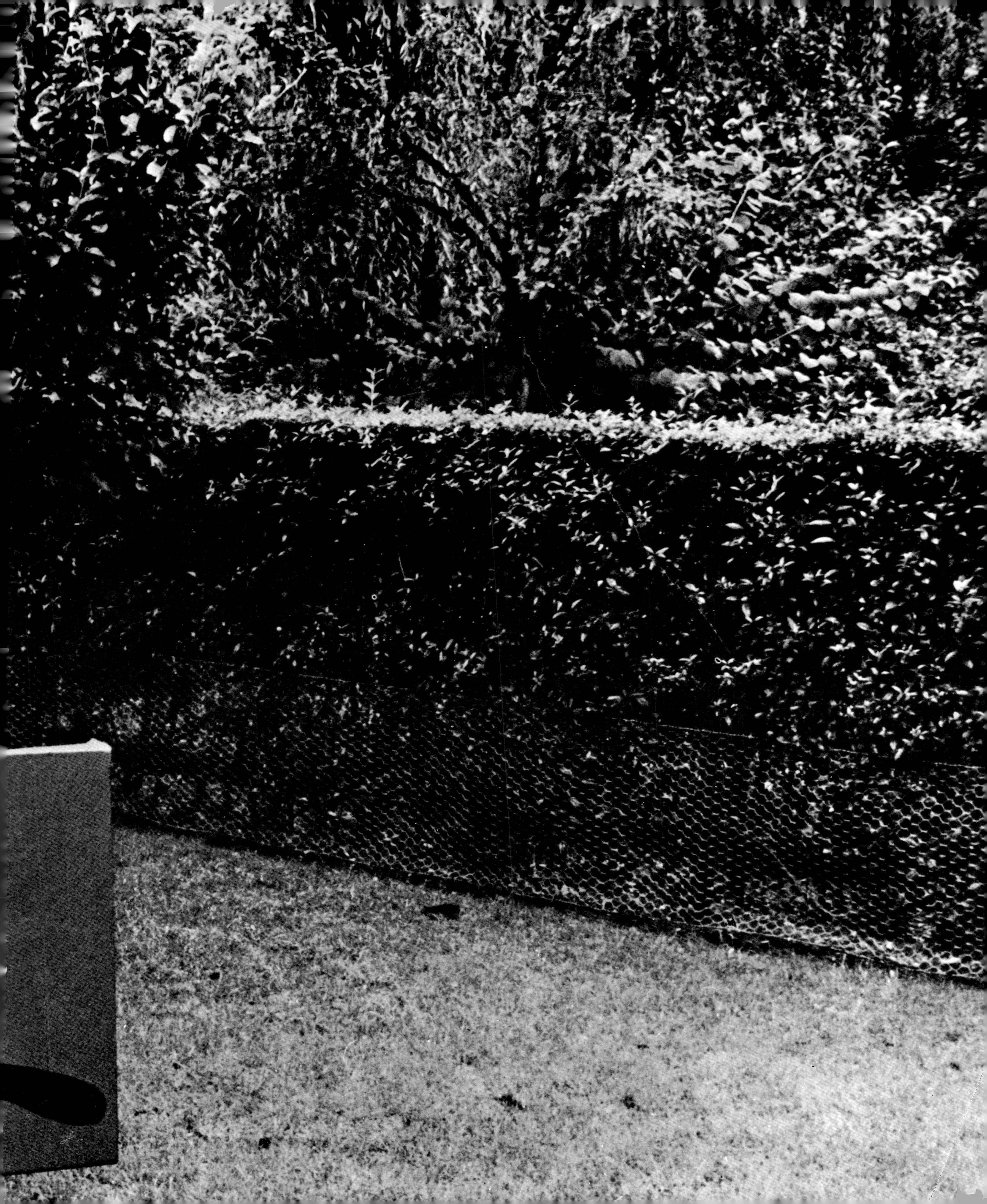